Words'
Worth

A STEP-BY-STEP TEXT FOR FEATURE WRITING

Words'
Worth

Write Well and Prosper

SECOND EDITION

Terri Brooks
Weill Cornell Medical College

Mary Quigley
New York University

WAVELAND
PRESS, INC.
Long Grove, Illinois

For information about this book, contact:
Waveland Press, Inc.
4180 IL Route 83, Suite 101
Long Grove, IL 60047-9580
(847) 634-0081
info@waveland.com
www.waveland.com

10-digit ISBN 1-57766-677-1
13-digit ISBN 978-1-57766-677-6

Printed in the United States of America

7 6 5 4 3

To Terri's son Brian
To Mary's children: Brendan, Sean, and Colleen

About the Authors

Terri Brooks is Director of Communications for the Office of Institutional Advancement at Weill Cornell Medical College in New York City. She began her career in communications as a reporter, feature writer, and columnist at the *Chicago Tribune*, followed by several years as a full-time successful freelance writer for major magazines and newspapers. She was for 13 years a journalism professor and then chair of the Department of Journalism at New York University, until she was recruited to serve as dean of the College of Communications at Pennsylvania State University. During the first wave of Web development she left academia to create the consulting firm Brooks New Media, which provided writing, marketing, and media advice to start-ups in Soho and Silicon Valley, and to major corporations such as Ameritech (now AT&T). She served for several years as writing coach for DuPont, media analyst for the Consulate-General of Japan in New York, a judge for the National Magazine Awards, and on the board of the Fulbright Association. Before her current position, she was Director of Communications for Development at New York University's Langone Medical Center. Terri is the author of three nonfiction books. She received her BA from the University of Wisconsin–Madison and her MA from St. John's College, Annapolis, Maryland.

A faculty member at New York University's Carter Institute of Journalism, Mary W. Quigley teaches graduate and undergraduate courses in basic and advanced news writing, feature writing, magazine article writing, and writing for the Web. She has worked as a newspaper reporter, freelance magazine writer, and is the author of two books about women and work. She ventured into digital media with a beat blog, mothering21.com, which covers "parenting" children over age 21. She received her BA in English from Fordham University and her MA in journalism from New York University.

Contents

Acknowledgments

Terri Brooks thanks those friends and colleagues who through their support in so many ways assisted with the first and second editions: Elizabeth Abrams, Miriam Arond, Francoise and Sidney Aronson, Carole Ashkinaze, Andrea Barbalich, James Carey, Rondi Charleston, Roy Peter Clark, Judith Daniels, Edwin Diamond, Jill Drew, Kingsley Ervin, Jeanne Lamb, Betty Medsger, James H. Ottaway, Jr., Eileen Alt Powell, David Rubin, Jerry Sass, Paula Span, Paul Steiger, her first publisher St. Martin's Press, and our new publisher Waveland Press, which has given this book its third lease on life. She also thanks the editors of her "hometown" newspaper, *The New York Times,* who through the decades have groomed and showcased some of the country's most talented feature writers, providing inspiration for thousands of students.

This edition, like the first edition, is dedicated to her son, Brian Brooks, who has grown from infancy to adulthood, thrived, and developed his own wonderful way with words since this book first made its appearance.

Mary W. Quigley thanks her NYU colleagues and other writers, editors, and friends for their suggestions, including Jessica Alverson, Mohamad Bazzi, Jason Boog, Gary Belsky, Cora Daniels, Jonathan Dube, Frankie Edozien, Frank Flaherty, Rebecca Fox, George Freeman, Beth Harpaz, Tim Harper, Eve Heyn, Ruth Hochberger, Keith Kloor, David Kushner, Lynn Langway, Yvonne Latty, Betty Ming Liu, Thomas Lueck, Gregg McLachlan, Pamela Noel, Kenneth Paulsen, Adam Penenberg, Sonia Jaffe Robbins, Adam Rose, Philip Rosenbaum, William Serrin, Fran Stern, Vivien Orbach Smith, Patrick Thornton, Chandra Turner, and Paige Williams.

A Special Thank You to Our Students

We especially want to acknowledge our students. As teachers at New York University—and also, for Terri, as a teacher and dean of the College of Communications at Penn State University—over the years we found ourselves humbled, amazed, and inspired by the way students learn to write. Many had innate writing talent that taught us a thing or two about the power and possibilities of words. Those who struggled made us appreciate the difficulties of writing well. In feature writing classes at NYU, students wished aloud for years for a book that laid out for them a blueprint of the elements of nonfiction prose. There were good books on the market, but none seemed to suit. After 12 years of waiting in vain for someone else to write this kind of book, Terri finally wrote the first edition in 1989. It gives us both pleasure to know that it continues to be available in this revised second edition.

Introduction

First, a word.

This book is about the kind of nonfiction known as feature writing. The term "feature" covers a wide range of nonfiction writing: profiles and portraits of the odd, the famous, the obscure; coverage of war, disaster, tragedy, and celebration; investigative reporting; "how-to" stories; writing on trends, travel, fashion, music, and art.

Features vary in length—from a hundred words online to thousands of words in a magazine or book. Whatever the subject and medium, the common denominator of features is that they are usually about current issues; they involve careful reporting and research; and they depend on the strength of their writing to get themselves read.

In the past, feature stories were considered the soft underbelly of the "real news," as if they could not compete with the hard-muscled facts of journalism. Ironically, the feature techniques described in this book now drive journalism as well. They add depth and perspective. They anchor the flight of events.

Today, the best news stories incorporate components of the feature—an engaging lead, lively verbs, description, anecdotes, and a story made compelling not only because of the information conveyed but also because of the words used to convey it.

With the new channels of communication made possible by digital technology, more opportunities than ever before are open to feature writers. There's just one problem: good writers are harder than ever to find. That's where you—and this book—come in.

The Lead

In a straight-news story, the standard *inverted pyramid* lead still wears well: the most important five *W*'s appear first— Who, What, When, Where, Why—with the remaining information presented in descending order of importance. This "just the facts" approach to reporting fires, wars, murders, stock market plunges, and the other nitty-gritty upon which news thrives serves up the essential details quickly and clearly.

But the lead for a feature story—whether found online or in print—imposes other demands on the writer. It must lure readers into a story that they might otherwise ignore.

Feature leads are tough to write; they need to be wrestled to the mat. If not kept in control, they tend to degenerate into turgid prose, leaving the reader slogging through quicksand before finally reaching the hard ground of a salient fact.

The trick is to be clever and creative, without being schmaltzy or sloppy. Avoid worn-out clichés, predictable puns that make people groan, platitudes, and careless language in general.

Consider this array of failed leads:

The Tasteless. On a story about an infant abandoned just before New Year's Day: "While most people were preparing to ring out the old, someone rang out the new this week. . . ."

The Puzzling. On a story about a utility company rate hike: "The old saying that the grass is always greener on the other side of the fence isn't necessarily true when it comes to utility rates."

The Absurd. About an ethnic community: "Cleveland Ukrainians know great strides are taken in little steps."

1

Remember that the feature lead is the key that unlocks the story. It should hold promise; it should intrigue and tantalize. Keep in mind, too, that most people read a feature to the end not only because the subject may be of interest. It is the way in which the story is *told* that infuses it with life or condemns it to death.

How long should your lead be? In features of up to 750 words, the lead may run from one sentence to a brief paragraph. Avoid longer leads when possible (and it is usually possible). Don't waste space with a windy hello. Short paragraphs are easier on the eyes and less daunting to readers, both online and in print.

Save longer leads for feature articles of 1,000 words or more. First, the reader will recognize that this is a "long read" and will be more willing to settle into a good lead without losing patience. Second, whether online or in print, longer articles usually include more graphics, wider columns, and more art, so the eye is not besieged by a dense mass of type. But don't dawdle with your lead, no matter what your story's length. Make every word work.

Obviously, each lead is uniquely tailored to fit the story it introduces. In that sense, there are as many kinds of leads as there are features. But most leads can be identified as one of six basic varieties:

1. Anecdotal   4. Summation
2. Descriptive 5. Tease
3. Quote   6. Zinger

The kind you choose is to some extent predetermined by the subject, and your point of view toward that subject (see chapter 6 for more on point of view). A feature should not only inform, but also evoke reaction: touching, sad, funny, wistful, annoying, intriguing, outrageous, revolting. The aim is to elicit any of the constellations of emotion that reflect human foibles, failings, fascinations, and frustrations. The success of your lead depends on your diligence as a writer, your patience, your instincts about

2

what will work best, and the depth of your reporting. The longer you work at it, the better your odds for success.

Anecdotal

The anecdotal lead draws the reader into the feature with a revealing "mini" story that reflects the larger story at hand. It captures the article's theme in such a compelling way that readers want to read on.

Example 1

The coverage of disaster—whether earthquake, war, flood, or disease—is most effective when it spotlights the impact on one person, one family. Here is an anecdotal lead to a feature about the first days of the war in Iraq:

> The melancholy wail sailed across the city and pierced the walls of the middle-class Baghdad home. The sleepless family listened in silence until the mother, her face lined with fear and pain, shook her head.
>
> "Siren," she whispered.
>
> At that, her daughter jumped up and threw open the door. She ran to open the windows next, fearful the blast would shatter them. The son sprinted outside, hoping to spot a low-flying cruise missile that would send the family huddling, yet again, in a hallway.
>
> And they waited for the bombs.
>
> "It's terrible," the mother said, as the minutes passed. "We really suffer, and I don't know why we should live like this."[1]

Why It Works

If a feature contains conflict between two or more opposing camps, an example of that tension can be shaped into an effective anecdotal lead. In this case, a personal moment of fear crystallizes the drama: how a family in Baghdad reacts to the fear and threat of attack.

The writer freezes a moment in time and space: a family at home in bed one evening, the wailing siren, the rush to protect life and home, the wait for the missile strike. The writer sketches *just enough* detail to show the tension: the sleepless family, the daughter opening the door and windows, the son sprinting outside, the mother's quiet lament. The lead is stripped to the basics. The author could have inserted more quotes, more description, more background. By keeping it short and simple, it becomes more stark and powerful.

The sentence structure itself also enhances the tension intrinsic to the story. Sentences start "soft"—the sound of a "wail" that "sailed" as the family listened, the mother whispered. The sentences then leap into action just like the family, using verbs that vibrate with energy—jumping, running, sprinting, huddling. Then, in the silence waiting for the explosion, the sentences become quiet again. They wait. Minutes pass. Finally, for the first time, words of anger and fear are spoken.

Example 2

An anecdote need not be dramatic to qualify as a good lead, as long as it moves readers quickly toward the drama or scope of the story. For instance:

> Monday was a routine day for Grant Di Mille and Samira Mahboubian, the owners of the Street Sweets food truck, a mobile trove of croissants, cupcakes and cookies that got rolling last month.
>
> The couple loaded the truck by 6 a.m., parked in front of the Museum of Modern Art at 7, traded hostilities with other vendors from 9 a.m. to 1 p.m., and were surrounded by police officers by 2.
>
> "The police told these guys that nobody owns the streets. But it sure doesn't feel that way," said Mr. Di Mille. . . .
>
> In four weeks of business, the couple has been threatened at the depot where they park the truck; cursed by a gyro vendor who said that he would set their truck on

4

fire; told to stay off every corner in Midtown by ice cream truck drivers; and approached by countless others with advice—both friendly and menacing—on how to get along on the streets.[2]

Why It Works

This begins as a "puff piece"—a day-in-the-life story about a food cart vendor. In the first sentence, the writer creates a placid, reassuring moment, reinforced with a few pleasant descriptions: a vendor called "Street Sweets," the names of a few tempting pastries. In the second sentence, she turns the story on a dime: with the words "hostilities" and "police officers" she takes us into a U-turn and sends us in a less friendly direction.

The verbs—simple, sometimes passive in the first sentence—grow stronger to reflect the menace. The writer taps into the ironic nature of the story—a literal food fight—and uses the anecdotal lead as the engine that lets the story propel itself.

From here, the skirmish expands: fans of individual vendors weigh in on Twitter, Facebook, and blogs. Nonfood vendors jump into the fray. This lead, so unassuming at first, effectively draws the reader into a lively story of politics, immigrants, and the variables of urban living.

Descriptive

Nonfiction writers know that one good word is worth a thousand pictures. The descriptive lead is that "one good word," the verbal photograph that captures the essence of a person, a place, an event. While the anecdotal lead moves the story forward through time, the descriptive lead anchors the story in place. The challenge to the writer is to find the description that symbolizes an entire story. The good descriptive lead, like the anecdotal lead, is a powerful way to enter a story. It employs a basic rule of good writing: Show Don't Tell.

Example 1

Here is the lead to a profile of Evel Knievel, the motorcyclist who in the 1970s was famous for his death-defying leaps over rows of Mack trucks and Greyhound buses.

> The old daredevil tips back in his recliner, nursing a blue lollipop. His small white dog, Rocket, slumbers in his lap. On the Food Network, a chef is shouting. Evel Knievel grabs the remote, fumbles with the buttons. "Blasted thing," he growls. "I can't turn it down." He slams the clicker on the table beside him. Buries his face in his hands. "I spend my days right here, mostly," he says, without lifting his head. It's been three weeks since his second stroke. He is always tired, sometimes addled. Knievel is 68 but has the body of—well, of a man held together with pins and plates. "I used to go all over the world," he grumbles. "I used to travel eight months a year. Now I can't even drive."[3]

Why It Works

The writer uses detail to play off the present against the past. She selects specific, tangible actions that convey the complex emotions—fatigue, frustration, anger, despair—of a sick, housebound man who once enjoyed superhero status. Rather than telling the reader *about* Knievel's physical decline, she *shows* the facts that reflect the decline and its emotional toll.

To do this, the writer takes advantage of three literary techniques used almost instinctively by feature writers.

First, *attention to detail.* Look for little things that most people miss or disregard as unimportant: the type of chair (recliner); the lollipop (perhaps medicated?); the name of the cable channel (Food Network) and who is shouting; the dog's name, "Rocket," an ironic echo of how Knievel was described in his glory days.

Second, *sensitivity to action.* Be aware of your subject's body language, no matter how fleeting: tipping back the chair; slamming down the remote because he can't control even that; burying his face in his hands while talking. Use body language, as this writer does, to convey emotion.

Third, *use of quotes and summary.* Use these selectively to reinforce the description. The quotes the writer selected reveal

6

a resigned frustration caused by Knievel's lack of mobility, especially in contrast with his past. After a few brief fact-filled sentences, the writer has established her own credibility. Now, she can swing into bigger picture summaries: about the strokes, the surgeries for broken body parts. She anchors the lead with the final compelling quote: "Now I can't even drive."

Example 2

This lead is on a second-day story about firefighters killed in a blaze that engulfed a furniture store in Charleston, South Carolina.

> Two-by-two, Charleston firefighters waded through the belly of the burning furniture store. Swirling black smoke choked the air around them and swallowed all light.
>
> Sofas, chairs and bedding blocked their path at every turn. Darkness and confusion enveloped the men. As the blaze turned deadly, calls for help crackled over the fire department's radios. One man prayed. From another: "Tell my wife I love her."
>
> Their tour of duty had come to an end. Nine lives. Gone.[4]

Why It Works

By the time readers look at the morning news, they often know from television and online sources the key facts surrounding a late-breaking major story from the day before. That was the challenge for these feature writers. Their solution was to put the reader at the scene during the last moments of the firefighters. To do this, they used the literary device of personification—attributing human qualities to abstract or nonhuman things—to make the scene of the fire apocalyptic: the firefighters are in the threatening "belly" of the store, like Jonah in the belly of the whale. The fire seems human as it "chokes" the air and "swallows" all light. The furniture store seems to come alive as it blocks their path of escape and shrouds the men in darkness. The reader becomes an eyewitness, sharing the men's intimate last moments and words. The sentences become shorter, faster like a heartbeat, and end with a single word: "Gone."

7

Quote

This kind of lead is used far more than it should be, often by writers who have given up on the lead and decide to throw in a quote just to get the story started. From time to time, however, the perfect, irresistible quote comes along that seems a natural for the lead. If you use direct quotes, it is best to keep them short. If the quotes run long, be sure they are carefully interspersed with description—however brief—to break them up. And remember that one of the surest ways to kill a feature is to lean on quotes—to over quote—whether in the lead or in the body of the story (see chapter 5).

Example 1

Here is the lead to a feature on driving lessons in the city.

"I would suggest," Bob Kousoulos says calmly to his driving student, Jules, "that you do something soon with the brakes. It is a red light, Jules."

"Jules, the brakes!"

Mr. Kousoulos, who has been teaching driving for 12 years and is a veteran of thousands of driving missions on the streets of New York, chain-smokes Marlboros, chuckles nervously and tries to maintain a veneer of calm.

"This pedestrian in the middle of the street," Mr. Kousoulos says softly as the vehicle picks up speed after the light, "has apparently decided to end it all. I know you have the right of way, Jules, but let her go, Jules—let her go!"

"Jules," he says, as the student driver weaves his way tensely through pedestrians crossing against the lights, through fields of potholes, numerous construction projects, bicyclists, triple-parked cars and other obstacles that make up the New York motoring experience, "I am sure that this man ahead likes his car, that he would prefer you not hit his car."

"Get into the next lane, Jules. Please!"[5]

8

Why It Works

This on-the-scene monologue effectively conveys the stress and humor of the situation. Through these one-sided quotes (we never hear the student's responses—he is the foil for this comedy routine) the reader senses barely averted disaster.

But good quotes need a good support system to be effective. This has it. *Punctuation* and *paragraphing* play a big role in pacing the monologue to heighten tension and humor: commas, exclamation marks, and a dash all make it feel as if the reader as well as the car is moving ahead in jerky fits and starts. And the two truncated paragraphs, each containing a single alarmist quote ("Jules, the brakes!" and "Get into the next lane, Jules. Please!"), are like brakes themselves, pulling the reader up short before lurching ahead to the next crisis.

Description is placed strategically to highlight the quotes and the tension. At each crisis, the ongoing quote is interrupted by description—the teacher chain-smoking, the car speeding up, the obstacles in the road—leaving the reader suspended briefly in the face of near disaster.

The descriptions themselves are vivid, to the point. They are the setting in which the jeweled quotes are placed, and each description is intended to enhance the impact of the quote. Specific word choice also lends a tragicomic effect. The teacher is a "veteran" of "missions," as in war. This is "the New York motoring experience," which sounds straight out of a 1920s tourist guidebook. In addition, the repetition of the student's name—seven times in this brief space—emphasizes the frazzled nerves of the anxious instructor.

Example 2

One advantage of quotes is that they can take the reader directly to the heart of a story, into the most bizarre and private corners of the soul, without seeming to be intrusive.

Here is the quote leading to a story of a private paramilitary training camp for mercenaries.

"I want to talk to you today," Frank Camper says, "about removing ears."

Mr. Camper, surrounded by his bruised and bandaged students, demonstrates the slap, grip and downward twist that is the recommended method for separating an ear from its owner during a fight. "After you've got it, the man won't believe it," Mr. Camper says. "So take a step back . . . and show it to him."[6]

Why It Works

An act that to most people is abhorrent, to this man is a matter of pride. For this reason, the author apparently couldn't resist using it in the lead. In this case, it was appropriate: the lead was but the first of many examples of the camp's gung-ho enthusiasm for brutality. But if you use a "shocker" quote such as this, be sure it is a fair reflection of the tone and information in the rest of the story.

Summation

The summation lead is comparable to a straight-news lead because it gives the basic information up front. Like the direct quote lead, it may be a sign that the feature writer simply gave up on finding a more creative way into the story. Sometimes, however, it is a simple and effective way to begin.

Example

In the children's clothing industry, there's a lot more to sexual identity than pink and blue. Starting with sleepsuits for the newborn, a child's gender is broadcast by a full code of design details. A former freelance designer for Babytogs, which distributes in K-Marts across America, cited some examples: "Round collar for a girl, pointed for a boy. Scalloped edges—never on a boy. For appliqués, trains and soldiers for boys, never flowers. A cat is a girl, a dog is a boy. Butterflies girls. Hot dogs are for boys, and ice cream cones for girls. And the bottom line is—Never Put Fruit on a Boy's Garment."[7]

Why It Works

Because the subject matter itself is about a frivolous and arbitrary practice, it is almost as if the author is determined

10

not to succumb to the same frivolity. This is, in fact, written in a tone similar to that used to cover fashion shows: here's what's new on the scene this season. And because the lead (and the story itself) is written in such matter-of-fact straight-news style, it highlights the absurdity of the subject matter.

When using a summation lead, remember to follow the same rules used in a straight-news piece. Tell the reader immediately what the story is about, clearly and concisely. Be direct. Work on the language so it is clear, but also be as creative as possible without interfering with the content. Use interesting verbs (here, "broadcast" is a good example). And when necessary, back up the information with a quote or partial quote, and with examples (in this example the writer managed to combine both in a quote). If you are having trouble finding the "perfect lead" for your feature, the basic summary lead is often your solution.

Tease

Sometimes leads that pack the biggest wallop contain a conundrum, an intentional ambiguity, a puzzle, an insinuation.

Tease leads move the reader obliquely into the story with puns, double entendres, a hint of mystery, or a new twist to a cliché. They often take longer to write, but they can give your feature a sparkling start.

Example 1

Here is a lead on a story about a habit that can cause friction:

> Anytime Anne Fishel and her family talk about behaviors that are out of bounds during family meals, they come back to the Yom Kippur Incident.[8]

Why It Works

This sentence promises to unlock an intriguing family secret, to share with us the kind of gossip that is so irresistible to human nature. The "Incident," however, turns out to be a twenty-first century breach of etiquette: the use of cell phones, Blackberries, and other portable communication devices at inappropriate times and places. The lead is about a guest at the solemn Jewish holiday meal of Yom Kippur who was "surreptitiously texting—and not just once or twice, but almost continuously, from the apple-squash soup to the roast turkey." The lead was the tantalizing appetizer into the entrée of the bigger story on some of the intrusive lapses of protocol caused by instantaneous communications.

Example 2

This lead promises one thing, but delivers quite another:

> There was romance in the resumés: She, a computer consultant turned fashion model; he, an Apple computer engineer turned Silicon Valley entrepreneur. They were young, beautiful and wired for love.
>
> But caution fell between them. During a yearlong courtship, Alfred Tom held back, wary of revealing too much. Then it happened. After an afternoon with his friend, Mr. Tom took Angela Fu back to his car. There, on the front seat of his 1994 Integra, he went for it.[9]

Why It Works

This lead promises romance. A proposal? A date? Sex in the car? Not so. The young businessman, it turns out, was asking his girlfriend to sign a nondisclosure agreement (NDA), so that she would be sworn to confidentiality about any trade secrets he might reveal during their intimate moments together. It was a perfect teaser lead on a story about the tight community of Silicon Valley, and the important role that NDAs play in the high-tech world.

In these two examples, you can see how powerful this approach can be for drawing readers into the net of a larger story that they might otherwise avoid.

Zinger

The zinger lead, which usually appears in light, humorous stories, is, like the tease, hard to write but satisfying to read. And like the tease, it often includes a massaging of the language into some slightly new configuration. Its unique quality is that it always includes a one-two punch. The reader is first set up, then nailed with a clever line.

One classic zinger lead appeared in the now-defunct Chicago *Daily News* after criminal Richard Loeb was stabbed to death in prison by an inmate whose sexual favors he had been soliciting. The story began: "Richard Loeb, who was a master of the English language, today ended a sentence with a proposition."

The lead, though it does qualify as tasteless, remains irresistible to punsters and grammarians alike.

With a zinger lead you can't take long to throw the punch: it must be hard and fast.

Example 1

Here is the headline: "What Has 132 Rooms and Flies?" The setup:

> The White House is bugged!

The punch:

> No, not like that. But actual flies are swarming the place, confounding housekeepers, irritating aides, even trying to feast on the president. During an East Room interview with John Harwood for CNBC and *The New York Times* on Tuesday, a giant fly orbited Mr. Obama's head.[10]

Why It Works

This is actually a double zinger. First, the headline ("What Has 132 Rooms and Flies?") is a play on the old fly joke:

Q: "What has four wheels and flies?"
A: "A garbage truck."

13

Second, the word "bugged," especially in the context of the White House, is assumed to be the term commonly used for electronic eavesdropping.

The story then goes into the causes of the flies, the projected solutions for getting rid of them, and the history of similar White House fly invasions that have bugged presidents past.

Example 2

While more commonly used in humorous features, the zinger can be a dramatic approach to serious stories as well. It can convey impending doom and heighten the poignancy of tragedy.

The setup:

> On autumn days, when the flaming aspen lit the nearby foothills golden, Christopher Mastalski did magical things with a football on the playing fields of Centaurus High School.
> He had that special mix of talent that the good running backs share: strength, balance, speed and an elegant grace.
> Had all gone well, 18-year-old Chris Mastalski would have played football for the University of Colorado next fall. Coach Chuck Fairbanks' staff ranked him among the top 20 prospects in the state.

The punch:

> Instead, the young athlete died Tuesday from knife wounds he had received the night before.[11]

Why It Works

Here, the lead dramatizes the contrast between the promise of vibrant youth and the tragedy of violent death. The writer introduces this profile with the imagery of life—flaming aspens, golden foothills, gifted athletic ability, elegant grace. The writer immediately makes us feel we would like this young man if we knew him, and this lure to familiarity is heightened when he refers to the subject initially by his more formal name, Christopher, and then, in the third paragraph, by his nickname, Chris.

But from the beginning, juxtaposed with all this vitality, are the verbs marshaled so relentlessly in the past tense, which convey a sense of doom.

Both the promise and the threat are there. And, in the fifth sentence, the writer takes away the young man, forever—that single, final fact cutting starkly across the page. The lead serves the story well, for it evokes first a glow of health and bounty, and then a shock of outrage, leaving us bereft.

EXERCISES

How good are you at writing leads? Here is a way to challenge and improve your lead-writing skills.

1. Find six feature stories that illustrate the six kinds of leads described in this chapter.

   a. If you find the lead to be effective, analyze why, using the same kind of analyses found in this chapter.

   b. If the lead is weak, rewrite it to make it better. You may alter the existing lead, or write an entirely new one.

2. Find a straight-news story of at least 500 words and write three feature leads for the story.

3. Find a magazine-style feature of about 1,500 words and address the following questions:

   a. What kind of lead is in the story?

   b. Does it "work"? If so, why? If not, why not?

   c. How could it be improved?

   d. Write three new leads for the story. Analyze which of the three works best, and why.

NOTES
[1] Anthony Shadid, *Washington Post*, March 24, 2003.
[2] Julia Moskin, *The New York Times*, July 1, 2009.
[3] Lane DeGregory, *St. Petersburg Times* (FL), August 5, 2007.
[4] Glenn Smith, Nadine Parks, and Noah Haglund, *Post and Courier* (SC), June 20, 2007.

[5] William Geist, *The New York Times*, November 28, 1984.
[6] Timothy K. Smith, *Wall Street Journal*, August 20, 1985.
[7] Jan Hoffman, *Village Voice*, April 17, 1984.
[8] Sara Rimer, *The New York Times*, May 26, 2009.
[9] Robert Frank, from *The Best Stories from* The Wall Street Journal*'s Middle Column*, Ken Wells, Ed. (New York: Simon & Schuster, 2002).
[10] Marc Leibovich, *The New York Times,* June 17, 2009.
[11] John Aloysius Farrell, *Denver Post*, March 4, 1982.

Transitions

Transitions are the words or phrases at the beginning of each paragraph that link one thought to the next. They sometimes occur within paragraphs as well, to link two sentences that contain disparate thoughts.

If transitions are successful, they lead the reader painlessly through even the most complex story. If transitions are inadequate, inappropriate, or nonexistent, the reader will feel befuddled and lost. When you need to reread an article, or parts of it, again and again to understand what is going on, the culprit may well be weak or ineffective transitions. However, transitions can't save an article that is poorly organized. It is important to structure your article with a logical flow from one point to the next. Then transitions can help make the structure seamless.

Transitions serve two purposes. First, they glue the story together, so it is cohesive. Second, they form a sequence of bridges to lead from quote to description to anecdote to background material without tripping over the junctures between ideas or information. The tighter a story, the better the transitions. The more complex a story, the greater the challenge to propel it along with strong, forceful transitions.

These two functions—to unify the feature, yet at the same time to move it in a new direction—gird the story. They provide the underlying shape, the skeleton upon which the flesh of the story hangs.

This ability to take command of a feature, to mold it and discipline it and coax the best performance out of each sentence, involves an act of aggression against words. You must control them and not let them control you. It takes time,

17

patience, determination, and experience to get your words to cooperate. But the longer you work at it, the more skilled you will become. As George Orwell warns, "In prose, the worst thing one can do with words is surrender to them."[1]

Beginning writers too often wait for inspiration, when they should be sweating over little things like transitions. Failure to discipline transitions is one reason why a feature with good potential may seem muddy. Fortunately, good editing can salvage a story that is suffering transition malnutrition. But the task is best done by the author.

Transitions should be short and unobtrusive. Usually, but not always, they are contained in short clauses at the beginning of the first sentence of the paragraph, like trailblazers marking the way. A good way to test the effectiveness of your transitions is to read the first sentence of each paragraph of your story. From them alone, you should be able to tell where you are going, and where you have been.

As with leads, transitions come in many shapes and sizes. However, most transitions fall within one of seven categories:

1. Time   5. Emphatics
2. Place   6. Pings
3. Mood Changers   7. Quotes
4. Repetition

Time

Common time transitions include: while, next, finally, following, at last, once, before, now, sometimes, often, today, yesterday, tomorrow (next week, year, etc.), meanwhile, then, until, after, at present, later. Or you can use a day of the week, a season, a date, an hour, a year, or any variation on these. For example:

- *Sometimes,* people ask for her autograph.
- *On that summer day eighteen months ago,* the trial began.

- *A decade ago,* most people were not as concerned about the environment.
- *Next* season, the football team will again face a series of tough opponents.
- *Meanwhile,* word of the tragedy spread like wood smoke over this western Missouri town.

Place

Place transitions can be general: nearby, down the road, across the street, back at the ranch. Or they can be specific, using the name of a town, street, store, or any place that adds local color to the piece. They can also include measurements, from meters to miles to light years. Place transitions are usually contained within prepositional phrases (a preposition followed by a noun or pronoun). Here are some examples:

- *Up ahead, the Snake River* spooled around a long, grassy bend and then out of sight.
- *Down the hall,* a cough rattles, someone moans, a hair dryer hums.
- *In the middle of the next cornfield,* a solitary streetlight glowed defiantly, a rebel flag tied to its pole.
- Anh Duy Nguyen sat *in the office* and talked of bankruptcy.
- *At Boone, Ames, Marshalltown, Cedar Rapids, and Clinton,* hundreds of people gather to cheer the train on.
- *At a buffet luncheon,* he holds court from a folding chair.

Mood Changers

These kinds of transitions help the reader shift psychic gears. They may modify expectations or emotions and may signal what is to come. They may limit, expand upon, deepen, soften, or justify an idea or an action. Many conjunctions or

19

adverbs are valuable mood changers. Common mood changers include: not only/but also, instead, and, so, actually, despite, because, if/then, on the one hand/other hand, besides, but, however, although (even though), as (just as), too, indeed, of course, still, yet, while, in addition to. The use of mood changers helps the writer present the complexities of a person or situation within a brief space. Here are some examples:

- *Yet* there is another side to the story.
- *If* the economy improves, *then* the unemployment rate will decline.
- *But* they still want to go home for the holidays.
- *And* the police simply tried to hold their ground and keep the violence from escalating.
- *Because* cell phone sales have increased, the number of landlines has declined.
- *On the other hand,* Joe did not want to leave the club.
- *Despite* such assurances, residents say they will continue their opposition.
- *Not only* did the marathon runner finish in record time, she also raised the most money for the charitable cause.

Repetition

The general rule of thumb for transitions is: the briefer, the better. The transition should be innocuous, not intrusive. And sometimes the most effective way to move the story forward is simply to repeat a key phrase—usually a proper noun or pronoun—from time to time. A single word or phrase may be repeated, or the repetition may consist of varied but related words. This is especially useful in profiles.

In long features that contain lots of description, information, and quotes, the repetition of a person's name as a transition may not be at all noticeable, and may be enough to lubricate the story and keep it running smoothly.

Example 1

A feature story profiled a woman, Jean Kline, who died of heroin, and her twin sister, Beth, who survived her. The names of the sisters or other personal references to them are repeated over and over as transitions from one paragraph to the next; yet the reader doesn't notice why this feature is so easy to read. You can, in fact, get a good idea of what the story is about by reading only the first sentence of each paragraph—a sign that the feature is well constructed.

1. *Jean Kline* was a child of the working class. . . .

2. *Jean and Beth* were fraternal twins. . . .

3. The physical likenesses formed a bond between Jean *and Beth.*

4. *Jean* was adventurous, a tomboy given to taking dares.

5. Walter bought *Jean* a bow for their hunting expeditions.

6. *Jean's taste* for adventure took other forms.

7. *Beth* excelled in her studies. . . .

8. *The twins* moved in different circles.

9. *In both girls'* circles, drugs were easily obtained.

10. And heroin was "over the line," *Beth* said.

11. Graduating from high school in 1969, *both girls* found jobs.

12. *She* returned to her mother's house in October 1973 for the birth of *Beth's* first child.

13. And, by the start of the new year, *Jean* had gone over the line.

14. Years later, *Jean* would tell her friends about her introduction to heroin.

15. "You'll never understand," *Jean* told Johnson. "There's nothing like it."[2]

The beauty of being able to use repetition for transitions is that it keeps the story "clean" by reducing the volume of words that might otherwise be needed to help propel it along.

Repetition need not be confined to nouns or proper nouns. Any thoughtfully chosen word will do—but be careful. It is more common for writers to repeat words through neglect rather than through a deliberate plan to enhance the story.

However, well-planned repetition—of words or sentence structure—is a traditional rhetorical device and handy literary tool.

Example 2

Here is a feature on a family doctor who has just retired. The author speculates on why this physician in Greensboro, North Carolina, is so beloved by his community. She emphasizes the answers with the repetition of sentence structure—in this case, a subordinating conjunction. Notice, too, that these are all sentence *fragments,* which also helps to set them apart from the rest of the story.

- *Because* when Wake Forest scores a touchdown, he marches around the living room singing the Deacons' fight song.
- *Because* it never occurred to him to remove the photographs of his children's old flames from his office walls.
- *Because* he has told the story of his father getting rheumatic fever in the trenches during World War I so many times that his family can repeat each word and each pause for effect, and it still sounds dramatic to him.
- *Because* he doesn't know how to say no to a call for help or to give up on anything or anyone who has earned his loyalty.
- *Because* no matter what his friends and family do or don't do or say or don't say, it's all right with him.
- *Because* he believed in his work and remained true to the principles on which it was founded.[3]

Emphatics

Emphatics offer an alternative to repeating the same word over and over. They are transitions that nail down the previous thought. Emphatics include: this, that, there, those, these, it, in fact, to say the least, such. They are often adjectives or pronouns, depending on their use in the sentence. For example:

- *Such* a negative reaction by the voters forced the senator to change his stand on the issue. Millions of pounds of *these* chemicals have reached the ground water in many ways.
- *It* is not the kind of attitude Parisians like much.
- *That* saddens 67-year-old Clyde Smith, who has cut hair for 53 years.

Pings

By adding "-ing" to a verb, you create what is called a verbal. They often look like verbs, but act like nouns (called gerunds) or adjectives (called participles). They make wonderful transitions, because the forward momentum set up by a verbal seems to swing the reader ahead into the sentence.

The following are some example of verbs used as nouns:

- *Designing* a lightweight but powerful laptop computer was a challenge. ["Designing" is the noun; "was" is the verb.]
- *Stealing* a trade secret isn't easy. ["Stealing" is the noun; "isn't" is the verb.]

Here are some examples of verbs used as adjectives:

- *Wearing* high boots and *carrying* long poles and burlap bags, law enforcement officers invaded homes, shops, and offices in Arizona and eight other states earlier this month. [Here, "wearing" and "carrying" are present participle forms of the verbs "wear" and "carry." They function as adjectives, modifying the noun "officers"; "invaded" is the verb.]
- *Sitting* in a steel hospital chair, his forehead scarred, the bandages and tubes still clinging to his skin, Darr talked

of dealing with his grief. [Here, "sitting" is the present participle form of the verb "sit" and functions as an adjective, modifying the noun "Darr"; "talked" is the verb.]

In each of these examples, the reader must reach far into the sentence before finding out what the sentence is about. This helps propel the reader into the subsequent sentence.

But beware. The present participle verb form can also be dangerous because it tends to get entangled in thickets of prose. When using any "-ing" form of a verb, watch your antecedents and your implications.

Avoid the ridiculous, such as, *"Nailing* down the tent, the dog followed him inside." (This says the dog nailed down the tent. It is called a dangling participle.)

Avoid the improbable, such as this published report: "Federal officials learned that the 10,000 employees at a government office building in lower Manhattan were drinking potentially unsafe water at least one month before *informing* anyone, Federal documents show." (This implies that 10,000 government employees conspired to hide the fact they were drinking polluted water.)

When used carefully, however, the present participle is a good transition, giving readers that little extra tug into the story.

Quotes

There are several advantages to leading into a new paragraph, and a new idea, with a quote. It forms a natural watershed from one thought to the next. It adds another perspective. It provides information and insight. It expresses a view (which may or may not agree with the view of the author) and it evokes a response. One of its strongest advantages as a transition is that the quote uses no extra words. But make sure it's not just a weak fill-in. Use only solid, valuable quotes that can stand on their own. (Even when used as a transition, the quote should always serve other purposes as well. See chapter 5.)

Example 1

The words of a rescuer are used to illustrate the effort to save 47 giant pandas from an earthquake that struck Sichuan province in China:

> "We play with them a lot, to try to ease their minds," said Wei Ming, a keeper. In the first days after the quake, "they were really sensitive to noise and were very nervous. They are much better now," Wei said as he wrestled a teething panda that was biting his kneecap.[4]

These quotes serve as a bridge to describe the details of the entire rescue effort, and the importance of pandas in the Chinese culture.

Example 2

A feature on the power of social media like Twitter to build small businesses uses a quote from an Internet analyst as a transition to the bigger story:

> We think of these social media tools as being in the realm of the sophisticated, multiplatform marketers like Coca-Cola and McDonald's, but a lot of these super small businesses are gravitating towards them because they are accessible, free and very simple.[5]

This quote is the bridge that leads to several examples of small businesses—a bed and breakfast, a sushi restaurant, an antiques store—that are successfully using these new technologies as a no-cost way to build a customer base.

Each of the above quote transitions stands on its own; each offers insight and perspective without adding extra words.

Whatever transitions you choose, keep them simple and unobtrusive. But keep them *in;* without them, your reader will be lost.

EXERCISES

1. Print out a long feature (1,000 words or more) that you find interesting and lively, and read it to the very end. Be sure it is nonfiction (not fiction or essay).

   a. Circle all the transitions used to move the story along.

   b. Identify each kind of transition.

   c. Analyze why the writer used these particular transitions.

   d. Identify paragraphs in which more effective transitions could have been used.

2. Choose a piece from your most recent nonfiction writing that includes fact-based research. It could be a feature story (published or unpublished), term paper, essay, or online posting.

   a. Circle your transitions.

   b. Identify each kind.

   c. Notice where you have wordy transitions, and reduce them to under four words where possible.

   d. Notice where you have inappropriate transitions, and change them.

   e. Locate where you lack transitions, and insert them if needed.

   You may find as you work on transitions that you will want to reorganize parts of your story. It means you are tightening and refining your work; you are editing yourself.

NOTES

[1] George Orwell, "Politics and the English Language." In *A Collection of Essays* (Fort Washington, PA: Harvest Books, 1981), p. 169.

[2] Stephen Braun, *Detroit Free Press*, February 6, 1983.

[3] Greta Tilley, *Greensboro News & Record* (NC), October 5, 1986.

[4] Jill Drew, *Washington Post*, June 15, 2008.

[5] Claire Cain Miller, *The New York Times*, July 22, 2009.

Verbs

> Please do not annoy, torment, pester, plague, molest, worry, badger, harry, harass, heckle, persecute, irk, bullyrag, vex, disquiet, grate, beset, bother, tease, nettle, tantalize, or ruffle the animals.
> —The San Diego Zoo

English is blessed with great verbs, as someone who loves animals and words demonstrated in the above sign posted at the entrance to the San Diego Zoo. Several commandments govern verb use in feature writing:

1. Never use weak verbs when strong ones will do.

2. Never use passive voice when active voice will do.

3. Never use the past tense when the present tense will do.

4. Never use big or awkward verbs when little ones will do.

5. Never use adverbs to shore up weak verbs.

6. Never carelessly switch verb tenses.

7. Never violate subject-verb agreement.

Let's look at these rules and, equally important, their exceptions. (And then we'll discuss the bane of all writers, the pronoun.)

Never Use Weak Verbs
When Strong Ones Will Do

Verbs can make or break a story. And nothing will break a story faster than a string of listless verbs. The main culprits are forms of the verbs *to be, to go, to do, to get, to have,* and *to make.* There is nothing wrong with these verbs per se. Far from it.

They are staples of our language. They are comfortable and familiar; they don't startle or disconcert. But too many, thrown around carelessly, will make readers feel like they are slogging through quicksand; when the drag becomes great enough, readers balk and stop. After all, if the writer has not been patient enough to sow the story with hardy verbs, then why should the reader muster enough patience to slog on?

Verb abuse is a sign that the writer may in fact be sloppy about word choice in general, so that the sentences suffer not only from verbal anemia but also from other kinds of neglect. The same writers tend to lean on vagueness and clichés, so that the story slowly sinks, unloved and untended, into the tepid purgatory where all such syntax deserves to go.

Whenever you feel stuck for a pithy verb, consult a thesaurus or dictionary. You may not find the perfect word but you will expand your creative thinking.

Keep It Moving

Strong verbs tend to be particularly important in sentences that contain description. This is because description, while crucial to the life of a story, also stops the forward progress of the story to focus on specific details that will give it depth and breadth. To overcome this slowed momentum, it is useful to wrap description around action verbs to keep the story moving.

Here is an example of a stalled description:

> She *is* small and frail and *wears* a tattered red dress. She *goes* over to the child, *bends* down, and *picks* him up.

The problem here is that the first sentence contains all description, and no action. The second sentence plods along behind with weak verbs. To correct this, it can be rewritten:

> The tattered dress *clings to* [or *shifts loosely on*] her frail body as she *bends* to *pick up* the child.

In this edit, three weak verbs are cut: "is," "wears," and "goes." They are replaced with one new verb—"clings"—that

28

describes a more graphic *action*. By folding the description from the first sentence into the action of the second sentence, the story no longer stalls. Instead, the description becomes an unobtrusive part of the action.

Verbs are a powerful tool when used to enhance an already dramatic scene. When a teenager killed her parents, the reporter re-created the terror with careful description wrapped around riveting verbs.

> The first bullet *hit* Jean Turnmire in the left breast. "Ginger, I love you," the woman said as her 15-year-old daughter *squeezed* the trigger again.
>
> The second shot *struck* the left side of the woman's head, *killing* her instantly and making the third bullet, which *slammed* into her back as she *slumped* forward on her bed, unnecessary.
>
> J. S. Turnmire, *hearing* the gunshots in the back of the house, *leaped* from his easy chair in the den and *began running* towards his wife's bedroom.
>
> He *made* it to the hallway.
>
> There, a single bullet *hit* him in the left nostril, *ripping* apart the lower half of his brain.[1]

This brutal scene becomes even more unforgettable when described with the arsenal of verbs: hit, squeeze, strike, kill, slam, slump, leap, run, rip. It would have been less awful if the reporter had simply written a straight news story: "According to testimony, Mrs. Turnmire *was shot* three times. Her husband *was shot* once while trying to come to her aid."

Instead, the re-creation of the gruesome moment with the compelling verbs that heighten the massacre makes this an unforgettable scene—as much as one might like to forget it.

Spark Interest

But it is the undramatic moments—the ho-hum scenarios of everyday life—that provide the real challenge in verb use. Here the writer's ingenuity is put to the test. Trying to insert

29

verve into a political luncheon, a public relations event, a grand opening or ground-breaking; trying to spice up the profile of a person who is uncooperative or boring—these are the features in which writers must pry out those verbs that may salvage the story.

Indeed, verbs can save the writer who is faced with the formidable task of trying to make people and events look more interesting than they really are.

Here is how one reporter handles a public relations birthday party for singer Jerry Lee Lewis, a pioneer of rock and roll, held at a bar in Memphis, Tennessee:

> Invitations in hand, his friends *surged* into Hernando's Hideaway, a wood-paneled juke joint on Memphis' south side, to *get liquored up* and to *party* all night long last Monday. . . .
>
> *Squeezing* around his table, they *jockeyed* for his attention. Big-boned, hulking farmers *vied* with publicity men in leisure suits to *shake* his hand. Bored young women in leather and chiffon *pressed* against giddy middle-aged ladies with beehive hairstyles to *take* snapshots and *peck* him on the cheek.[2]

Every verb is pulling its weight here; every verb carries momentum. Not because the story lends itself to these particular verbs, but because the writer finds the verbs and lends them to the story. The less experienced writer might have written it this way:

> Several hundred people *came* to Hernando's Hideaway, a wood-paneled juke joint on Memphis' south side, to *have* a good time and *try to shake* the hand of Jerry Lee Lewis. The people there *ranged* from big-boned, hulking farmers to publicity men in leisure suits, from bored young women in leather and chiffon to giddy middle-aged ladies with beehive hairstyles.

This is the kind of prose often produced by beginning writers—a prose not yet sensitive to the power of verbs. The problem in this second example is that all the action occurs in the first sentence; the second sentence contains only description. So the writer has two tasks here: first, to integrate the action and description; second, to beef up the verbs. Why use limp

30

verbs like "have," "try," and "range" when lively verbs like "surge," "liquor up," "party," "jockey," and "vie" are available?

Compress Action

Effective use of verbs depends not only on your mastery of the subtleties of the English language, but also on your perceptiveness in gathering the kinds of description that can be wrapped effectively around verbs (see chapter 4). If you are observant enough, you can insert action in places where, to the untrained eye, no action seems to tread.

For example, the gentrification of a neighborhood over several years does not on the surface lend itself to zippy verbs. But this writer achieves time compression by using apt verbs and tight transitions (see chapter 2).

> One day, there was an empty space at the corner of Stark and 79th. The next, a man with a mustache *slammed* a sledgehammer, clearing space for a coffee shop. Then *came* the echoes of demolition from the old theater, dormant for years. Another day, the neighborhood *woke up* to a wine bar.[3]

These few verbs are the written equivalent of a visual fast-forward, where a day's worth of clouds seem to fly by in seconds, and a new building goes up in a minute.

And here, for example, is a profile of a train announcer at Pennsylvania Station in New York City, a man whose sedentary job is to sit in a booth all day long and call out train arrivals and departures.

> He *sits* alone in a darkened Plexiglas booth that *juts* from the wall 10 feet above the floor of the main waiting room. One day this week, a commuter *leaned* against a post and *waited* for Mr. Simmons to *bellow* his next "All aboard!", then *gave* him the thumbs-up sign and *hustled* off to work.

31

> An elderly woman *waited* for an "All aboard!", then *blew*
> Mr. Simmons a kiss and *was* on her way.
> Up in the booth, Mr. Simmons *barked* out the last call
> for The Crescent. An elderly couple *applauded.* A young
> couple *held* each other in a fast embrace. A young man
> *crashed* through the crowd, *racing* for the train, and several
> commuters *charging* to another train *sang* out the "All
> aboard!" in chorus with Mr. Simmons.[4]

This job is basically boring, as Daniel Simmons himself
pointed out to the writer. So the writer finds ways to compensate. First, he uses strong verbs when describing Simmons's
work. His booth doesn't just stick out or protrude from a wall,
it assertively *juts* out; Simmons doesn't just announce loudly,
he *bellows,* he *barks.*

Second, the writer spices up the story by including others'
reactions to Simmons's voice. By focusing on a few moments
in a given day, and by watching carefully, the writer is able to
capture the kind of detail that lets him incorporate more zest—
people lean, hustle, blow, applaud, hold, crash, race, sing—
into an essentially quiescent story. Because the writer captures
these responses *from* others, rather than relying on Mr. Simmons's response *to* others, the writer has managed to work his
way around the story until he finds an "in" for action verbs.

In fact, no matter how quiet a moment, a good writer can
capture it with compelling, assertive verbs. Here, for instance,
is how one writer described a widow at a memorial service for
her husband.

> Her head *fell* forward as the bugler began to play, her hair
> *covered* her face like a curtain, and her face *folded* like paper,
> and then she *raised* her head, *swung* the hair back, almost
> defiant in her determination to face up, to be strong.[5]

The untrained eye might see only a woman sitting quietly, a
look of grief on her face. This writer notices the small details,
and then couples them with a series of verbs that indicate first
a closing in upon oneself, a descent into grief—"fall," "cover,"
"fold"—and then a tentative spark of strength, of tenacity,
with verbs like "raise" and "swing."

32

Never Use Passive Voice
When Active Voice Will Do

When carelessly used, the passive voice slows the pace of the story. When verbs are active, so is the sentence. When verbs are passive, the sentence also loses its punch: instead of doing something, the subject has something done *to* it. For example:

Active: She *passed* the salad around the table.

Passive: The salad was *passed* around the table.

When a sentence is in the passive voice, we don't know *who* is performing the action. The actor is missing, unknown unless a phrase is added.

The impact of the passive voice is to wind the sentence back upon itself, so that instead of moving forward it seems to be elliptical, with the verb guiding the reader backward toward the subject of the sentence rather than onward to the object.

But be forewarned—verbs are feisty creatures, chafing at their barricades. In fact, much of what follows will deal with exceptions to this rule to favor the active voice. Nevertheless, the rule itself stands firm.

There are times, for instance, when the passive verb form is unavoidable, and even acceptable. It occurs often, for instance, when writers describe a legal action: she *was released* on bond; he *was read* his rights; police *were called* to the scene; court *was adjourned;* they *were promised* immunity.

While these examples could be converted to the active voice (the judge *released* her on bond; the police *read* him his rights; a telephone call *brought* police to the scene; the judge *adjourned* the court; the district attorney *promised* immunity) the change doesn't improve the copy, and can even seem awkward. Common usage wins out.

The passive voice also might be used when the subject is an unknown or amorphous "other"—whether an individual or a group. For example:

33

- Toxic wastes *were dumped* on his property about 20 years ago.
- Many proposals *have been offered* for a new stadium.
- In emergencies, food and supplies *are airlifted* to save lives.
- The government's plan to demolish the camp by the end of the year *has been deferred* for the time being.

It is understood in the above sentences that the strength of the sentence lies not in who performed the action, but in the potential *results* of the action—dumping toxic wastes, building a stadium, saving lives, postponing the demolition.

The passive voice is also a way to avoid inserting the reporter into the story. Consider this profile of a judge who is under attack for always ruling to overturn death penalty verdicts:

> The chief justice of the California Supreme Court *is asked* to imagine, momentarily, that she is gazing across her desk at the mother of a murdered child.

It would be intrusive for the reporter to write, "I ask the chief justice of the California Supreme Court to imagine. . . ." It would detract from the real subject of the story—the judge and her opinions. In this example, the passive voice keeps the writer in the background.

If you are really confident about your ability to control a story through verb use, the passive voice may also be used from time to time as a literary device to reflect a person's help-lessness or inability to control a situation.

One example is in this story about an elderly couple being harassed by teenagers:

> On a night around Easter, his house *was* bombarded with raw eggs.

Or in this story of a fatal accident about to happen during the filming of a movie:

> Behind them things *were blowing up,* brilliant, thudding, high cascades of light.

Each of these sentences has other strengths to compensate for the passive verb form. First, the verbs themselves are lively: "bombard" and "blow up." Second, the construction of the sentences compensates for the passive voice.

Let's look at the first sentence. It both begins ("On a night around Easter") and ends ("with raw eggs") with prepositional phrases that together absorb the weight of the sentence. The emphasis is at the beginning and the end, and the verb—the hostile action—acts like a hinge on which the sentence swings.

In the second sentence, the tension seems to rise slowly to a crescendo in the series of descriptions *beyond* the verb—"brilliant, thudding, high cascades of light." This combination of passive verb and delayed action makes the sentence seem to move in suspenseful slow motion—there is violence, but as seen from a distance, like a far-off bombing.

Or, you can deliberately use the passive voice to break out of a string of active verbs in order to alter the pace of the story. When you use passive verbs in this way, they also tend to highlight information that precedes or follows.

Here, for example, is how two writers describe U.S. Customs Service agents tracking a drug-laden plane from Colombia as it enters Florida airspace:

> Radios *begin to buzz* as voices *detail* the northward path of the plane. Agents *scramble* to *open* metal lockers and *pass out* flight bags. Pistols *are strapped* on belt loops. Handguns *are slipped* into shoulder holsters and boots. Shotguns *are filled* with shells.
>
> Pilots *huddle* over a maze of maps which *cover* the long route from Florida to an isolated, unlit airfield deep in the Pocono Mountains of Pennsylvania, where the target plane *is expected to land.*
>
> Bullet-proof vests *are handed out.* Half-smoked cigarettes *are crushed* into overflowing ashtrays. The agents *rush* out the door to their waiting planes.[6]

Out of the sixteen verbs used, more than one-third are passive. Yet the scene seems to crackle with action. Why? First, most of the verbs are small but powerful, and are in the present tense: buzz, scramble, strap, slip, huddle, cover, crush, rush.

The writer is also careful to bracket the entire scene with active verbs: the first two sentences and the last sentence are in the active, not the passive, voice (and have peppy verbs like buzz, scramble, rush). And notice how the passive verbs, with one exception, are confined to short, brisk sentences. That exception comes in the long single sentence in the middle paragraph, which helps to break up the repetitiveness of the short, snappy sentences in the first and third paragraphs. That long sentence also helps emphasize the action-packed shorter ones around it.

It is unlikely, of course, that the writers sat down and did a content analysis of the impact of using the passive voice in this scene. Rather, they had a sense of what "works" in their copy—an intuition about language that comes only with careful attention to word choice and syntax, an ability that improves with experience.

Consider how their story would flow if they had followed a hard-and-fast rule of using active voice only:

> Radios began to buzz as voices detail the northward path of the plane. Agents scramble to open metal lockers and pass out flight bags. They strap pistols on belt loops. They fill shotguns with shells.
>
> Pilots huddle over a maze of maps which cover the long route from Florida to an isolated, unlit airfield deep in the Pocono Mountains of Pennsylvania, where they expect the target plane to land.
>
> The supervisor hands out bullet-proof vests. Agents crush half-smoked cigarettes into overflowing ashtrays. They rush out the door to their waiting planes.

Not bad. It would pass most editors' desks. But the lack of variety in the verbs makes this less snappy than the original.

However, keep in mind that the above exceptions prove the rule. Only use the passive voice with intent—to produce a certain effect—and always use it with care.

When possible, stick to the active voice. It will get you there faster.

Never Use the Past Tense When the Present Tense Will Do

Writing in the present tense makes the story seem more immediate, as in the above example. Use it whenever possible. It particularly lends itself to profiles or "offbeat" features about places, people, or situations. If you do a feature on a local bakery, a profile of a politician, or an in-depth report of a controversy, it can be presented in the present tense as long as the bakery, politician, or controversy remain extant.

In this example, the reporter puts the reader inside a Florida classroom by using precise, present tense verbs that convey action and sound:

> It's endless, the things ninth-graders do to annoy.
>
> In class, they *chatter*. They *cuss*. They *whistle*. They make squeaky mouse noises. They *snork up* phlegm. They *burp* and *fart*, *interrupt* and *talk back*, *interrupt* again: "Sorry." They don't say the Pledge of Allegiance. They say, "That's gay." They *blow* bubbles—pop—and *blow* them again after being told not to. Pop! They *crumple* paper for maximum crunch. They *draw* penises on work sheets.[7]

The writer has total control of this story. He mined the deep vein of English verbs for maximum effect. None rings a false note. None is wasted. This kind of result takes long, hard work, and with enough practice and love of language, many feature writers can achieve this.

Never Use Big or Awkward Verbs When Little Ones Will Do

Awkward verbs come in several disguises. There are pretentious ones, silly ones, bloated ones. In general, the bigger the verb the more oblique its meaning. Short verbs tend to be more concise.

As the English language evolves, adjectives and nouns are sometimes made into verbs, such as "to supersize," "to network," "to finalize," "to fault," "to bus," "to hassle," "to room." These types of verbs seem jarring when they first appear, but some eventually become accepted in common usage. Business jargon has introduced "to bottom line," "to brand," "to outsource," and "to downsize," among others. The Internet has given us an irresistible array of convenient new verbs such as "to cyberstalk," "to stream," and "to friend."

Because language is malleable, and always in a state of flux, it is sometimes hard to know which of these "new" verbs will eventually enter mainstream English, and which will just fade away. H. L. Mencken, one of America's great prose stylists, complained way back in 1919 about many new verbs-from-nouns, such as "to contact," "to audition," "to curb," "to alert," "to package," "to research," and "to panic"—all of which are now standard linguistic fare. Mencken, who listed many that never made it to the end of the twentieth century ("to music," "to biography," "to siesta," "to guest"), also had this to say about verbs and their relatives:

> The nouns in common use, in the main, are quite sound in form. The adjectives, too, are treated rather politely, and the adverbs, though commonly transformed into the forms of their corresponding adjectives, are not further mutilated. But the verbs and pronouns undergo changes which set off the common speech very sharply from both correct English and correct American. This is only natural, for it is among the verbs and pronouns that nearly all the remaining inflections in English are to be found, and so they must bear the chief pressure of the influences that have been warring upon every sort of inflection since the earliest days.[8]

But if you are thinking of being creative and cute with verbs, a good rule to follow is: proceed with caution. An out-of-place noun or adjective used as a verb will probably detract from the larger story at hand. It is better to master the compendium of existing verbs before you start creating new ones. Read John McPhee (who cultivates verbs like "to parse," or "to seine") to get a sense of the big ideas that can come from small verbs. Keep it short. Keep it simple. Keep it moving.

Never Use Adverbs to Shore Up Weak Verbs

Avoid phrases like "speak softly" (just use whisper) or "move swiftly" (just use run, jog, trot, or dash, among others).

Writers unaware of the power of verbs tend to use adverbs where none are needed. In most cases, a strong verb is strong enough on its own; the adverb is redundant. A few examples from published stories include:

Verb/Adverb	Verb
wander away	wander
totally destroy	destroy
seriously consider	consider
wink slyly	wink
be absolutely sure	be sure
be definitely interested	be interested
be perfectly clear	be clear
mercilessly tortured	tortured

Use adverbs only when they add a descriptive ingredient to the story that a verb alone cannot supply:

He *viciously* attacked with a sharp chisel a three-ton block of limestone. [He could have attacked it hesitantly, skillfully, etc.]

He waits *nervously* for the guards to unbolt the first of several heavy metal security doors. [He could have waited confidently, calmly, etc.]

Never Carelessly Switch Verb Tenses

Ground your story in one tense. If you start your story in the present tense, stay there. If you start in the past tense, stay there. You can then use other tenses as needed to indicate corollary time changes in the story. Many beginning writers inadvertently change tenses in a feature. It is confusing for the reader, and will be caught by an editor (one hopes) before it goes to print. But editors slip up too. The ultimate responsibility for producing clean, clear, readable prose rests with the writer. If you frustrate and confuse your readers with inconsistent verb tenses, they will avenge themselves by turning to another story.

Never Violate Subject-Verb Agreement

Single subjects take single verbs; plural subjects take plural verbs. Once verbs start to wander from the vicinity of the subject, mistakes appear. Take, for example, these two stories that appeared in major newspapers:

> The very visibility that makes (her) the object of approving and consuming curiosity in the West *have* led to a broad feeling . . . that she is somehow overstepping her position. [It should be "visibility *has* led"]

> The official radio said his resignation from the leadership of the Burmese Government and the ruling party *were* accepted. [It should be "*was* accepted"]

These basic errors made it past some of the world's best editors.

One way to check on how well you are abiding by the seven verb rules given in this chapter is to go through your own story when you are done writing, and highlight your verbs. You will then be able to see if you have too many dull, passive, or overblown verbs, verbs shored up by superfluous adverbs, or errors in verb tense or agreement.

Verbs *alone* do not make or break a story, of course. Verbs are but one component—albeit an important one—in the complex, subtle, sophisticated machinery that constitutes a sentence, a paragraph, or a page of prose.

Once verbs start to wander from
the vicinity of the subject, mistakes appear.

But inattention to verbs usually indicates a general laxity about language. Only strong nouns, and a good sense of the heft of a sentence—how it will handle itself on the page—will compensate for shaky verbs.

Never Give In to Pronoun Misuse

We would like to add a word here about another common cause of writing glitches—the pesky pronoun. Writers need to be sure that the pronoun agrees with its antecedent. Every pronoun has an antecedent—a noun to which the pronoun refers. Your task is to be sure that if the antecedent is *singular,* then the pronoun is *singular* as well. For example: "The doctor claims her diagnosis is correct." Since the antecedent "doctor" is singular, then the pronoun "her" is also singular. If the antecedent is plural, then the pronoun must also be plural, as in: "The doctors claim their diagnoses are correct." This is not always as easy as it sounds, however.

The farther away the pronoun drifts from its antecedent, the greater the risk of error. This is especially true when other nouns intervene between the pronoun and antecedent. As in: "The doctors, after meeting with the lawyers, claim the diagnoses are correct and stand by their opinion. They know they must defend them if their doubts persist."

Who knows who must defend whom (or what) if whose doubts persist? This kind of muddle quickly leads to reader burnout. Few readers will attempt to untangle the pronouns and nouns—nor should they. It is the responsibility of the writer to do so. It would save confusion by simply rewriting it: "After seeking legal advice, the doctors know they must defend their diagnoses should doubts persist."

As linguist Jacques Barzun writes, pronouns inhabit a "dangerous wilderness. It is the duty of pronouns to be not wild but tamed, that is, tied down; yet their natural tendency is toward the jungle."[9]

41

The current endangered pronoun is "who." The correct pronoun when referring to people is either "who" or "whom." When referring to objects, the correct pronoun is either "that" or "which." For example:

- People *who* eat well tend to have more energy.
- Chairs *that* break can be easily fixed.

Today, people are often referred to in the same category as chairs and other inanimate objects, i.e., "People *that* eat well tend to have more energy." For some sensitive semantic souls, the misuse of this pronoun is like the sound of fingernails on a chalkboard. But there is no way to retrieve the unruly pronoun once it has broken through its corral.

In addition, because of the rules of English, some singular personal pronouns ("he/she," "him/her," "his/hers") lead to intrinsic sexism if not used with care. This problem exists in part because English lacks a unisex singular pronoun in the third person, such as the French "on." Our closest equivalent, "one," has a stilted quality to it that makes it an unacceptable substitute for "he" and "she." As a result, we commonly read inappropriately gender-specific writing. While parts of the English language live, breathe, and easily transform, other linguistic traditions die hard.

Limitations in the English language have also led to pronoun-created sexism. In early editions of *On Writing Well*, William Zinsser used only the male pronoun when giving advice to writers. He pointed out, for example, that:

> If a *reader* is lost, it is generally because the writer has not been careful enough to keep *him* on the path.[10]

His sentence is grammatically correct. The subject, verb, and personal pronoun are singular. But if the subject, "a reader," means "the average reader" or "the typical reader"—male or female—then the sentence is logically incorrect. The subject is non-gender-specific, while the pronoun is gender-specific. And let us assume that Zinsser did not intend to imply that the only readers who get lost are male readers. To correct the sexism, here are four possible solutions.

1. The sentence could say:

   If *readers* are lost, it is generally because the writer has not been careful enough to keep *them* on the path.

   While this is now grammatically and syntactically correct, it loses some of its punch to transform the example of one reader into all readers. A specific example is always better than a general one.

2. Or, the sentence could say:

   If a *reader* is lost, it is generally because the writer has not been careful enough to keep *him* or *her* on the path.

   This, too, is correct in its grammar and syntax, but the reader stumbles slightly over the double pronouns "him or her" near the end.

3. Another commonly used, though technically incorrect, option is:

   If a *reader* is lost, it is generally because the writer has not been careful enough to keep *them* on the path.

   The sentence is now grammatically a mess since the plural pronoun is referring to a singular antecedent.

4. The final option is to rewrite the sentence when possible, which is exactly what Zinsser did in a subsequent edition:

   "If a *reader* is lost, it is generally because the writer has not been careful enough."[11]

   This gets rid of the pronoun, and the problem, although it regrettably loses the apt metaphor about keeping readers on the path. But when it comes to clarity of language—whether grammatical or syntactical—this option seems to provide the least jarring solution.

EXERCISES

1. Here is a wire service description of a saloon on the edge of the Cheyenne Indian reservation in Jimtown,

Montana. Rewrite it to incorporate action verbs with the description.

> The saloon is a battered wooden building bearing vague evidence that it once knew paint. Its windows are screened with steel, of prison thickness. The sign over the door, "Jimtown Bar," is riddled with more than 100 bullet holes. The equally ventilated mailbox is the third replacement in less than a year.
>
> Come inside. A bar of raw oak runs the length of the room. In front of it are spaced 16 cottonwood tree trunks, each a foot and a half thick, smoothed by denim and gouged by knives. There is no other furniture. The bar rail is fastened not to the bar but to the tree trunks. . . . "I couldn't keep stools," Bob Edwards said. "They kept busting them over each other's heads."[12]

2. Find a feature that seems particularly bland. It could be about a person, a place, or an event.

   a. Circle all the verbs.

   b. How many of them would you classify as "dull" verbs (e.g., to be, to go, to do, to get, to have, to make)?

   c. How many are in the passive voice?

   d. Rewrite to reduce weak verbs and passive voice.

   e. Now highlight only the sentences that contain description.

   f. Rewrite those sentences where necessary, wrapping the description around stronger verbs.

3. Circle all the "dull" verbs in this chapter. (Or this book, for the more energetic.) How many can be replaced with livelier verbs? Rewrite as many of these dull verb sentences as you can.

4. The English language seems to conspire against the nonsexist use of pronouns, but avoiding sexism is possible through diligence and creative rewording. Rewrite this sentence to avoid sexism in pronoun use. "A shopper would have no way of knowing whether he was buying lettuce from California unless the manager knew,

and was willing to say, where his suppliers for this shipment were located."

5. The following examples contain one or more errors in agreement of subject-verb or pronoun-antecedent. Correct as necessary.[13]

   a. Is she one of the women who was picketing?

   b. Smithton Global ended the first attempt at selling their whole energy division late last year when they were unable to get "acceptable terms" from bidders.

   c. The House of Representatives voted against the bills because they were eager to recess.

   d. Has any of the statistics been released?

   e. Everyone on the boat knows that he will need to swim to shore.

   f. Read Plutarch's *Lives*. They will teach you about leadership.

   g. When a child is cranky, it usually means they are tired.

   Figure out your own answers first. Then read the following corrections and comments. Feel free to argue with them. Remember, English is a living, changing, challenging language.

   a. Here, the subject of a sentence is singular ("she") and the noun in the prepositional phrase between the subject and verb is plural ("women"). You may have been taught to ignore the prepositional phrase when deciding whether the verb following that phrase should be singular or plural. This rule, however, should not be followed slavishly. In this sentence, the clause "who was picketing" really describes all the "women" and not "she" or "one." The correct sentence is: Is she one of the women who were picketing? The sentence could also be rephrased: Is she among the women who were picketing?

   b. Companies employ many people, but in American usage the company itself is a single institution. So "it" is the proper pronoun in both places. The correct sentence is: Smithton Global ended the first attempt at selling its whole energy division late last year when it was unable to get "acceptable terms" from bidders.

c. The House of Representatives is a single institution but it's awkward to think of an institution as being "eager." Rather than automatically changing "they" to "it," it might make more sense to change "they" to a plural noun. A possibility: The House of Representatives voted against the bills because its members were eager to recess.

d. Again, look at what you are trying to say to the reader. If this is a situation where one statistic might be released, reword the sentence: Has any statistic been released? But if you are describing a case where some statistics (i.e., more than one) might be released, then the plural verb is correct: Have any of the statistics been released?

e. The grammatical rule that the pronoun "he" must be used following indefinite pronouns is no longer cast in stone. Possible alternatives to the false generic "he" are "he or she," or even "they," in some cases. But before automatically selecting a substitution ("he or she" seems awkward to many, and in this sentence "he and she" is more accurate), first see whether the sentence can be reworded. "They" would work here, and/or the noun could be changed: All on the boat know they will need to swim to shore.

f. *Lives* may be a plural word but in this case it is used as the title of a book. The correct sentence is: Read Plutarch's *Lives*. It will teach you about leadership.

g. Here, it isn't just some particular child who is cranky when tired. You're telling the reader that fatigue makes most children cranky. So change the singular in the first clause to a plural, and the rest follows naturally: When children are cranky, it usually means they are tired.

NOTES

[1] Susan Thomas, *Tennessean*, February 8, 1987.

[2] Stephen Braun, *Detroit Free Press*, October 2, 1983.

[3] Inara Verzemnieks, *Oregonian*, April 6, 2006.

[4] William Geist, *The New York Times*, January 5, 1985.

[5] Anna Quindlen, *The New York Times*, May 18, 1983.

[6] Susan Thomas and Joel Kaplan, *Tennessean*, July 19, 1982.

[7] Ron Matus, *St. Petersburg Times* (FL), December 10, 2006.

[8] H. L Mencken, *The American Language* (New York: Alfred A. Knopf, 1980), p. 526.

[9] Jacques Barzun, *Simple and Direct: A Rhetoric for Writers,* 4th ed. (New York: HarperCollins, 2001).

[10] William Zinsser, *On Writing Well* (New York: Harper and Row Perennial Library, 1988), p. 9.

[11] William Zinsser, *On Writing Well* (New York: Harper Collins, 2006).

[12] Jules Loh, *The Free Lance Star,* May 7, 1977.

[13] This exercise was developed by Sonia Jaffe Robbins, managing editor of *Publishers Weekly,* writer, and teacher. She is happy to answer your grammar usage questions on Twitter at http://twitter.com/warnfrcopyeditr

Description

Description is the lifeblood of the feature story. As Ernest Hemingway put it, "Experience is communicated by these small details, intimately preserved, which have the effect of indicating the whole."[1]

Three steps are needed to produce good description: (1) gathering it; (2) choosing how much of it to put in the story; and (3) deciding where to put it.

Most beginning writers need to work diligently on the first step—gathering description. No matter how brilliant their comprehension of the nuances of language, their copy often seems flat because they have failed to observe enough detail *at the scene.* As a result, they lack "color" for their feature.

Train Yourself to Observe

When gathering description, try to view the world without predilection. Put aside any biases that may distort what you see or impair your objectivity in the way you see it. Train yourself to notice *every* detail, like a painter; your palette is the paper upon which you will paint a word picture. Later, when you paint, you may choose to emphasize the warts, or glamorize the mundane. But as you collect information, withhold judgment, so that everything remains fresh and full of possibility. None of us can mentally record the barrage of sights, sounds, and smells that accost us all the time; there's simply too much to absorb. But we can train ourselves to notice these details while "on the job." Stephen Spender once said of fellow poet W. B. Yeats that

> he went for days on end without noticing anything, but then, about once a month, he would look out of a win-

dow and suddenly be aware of a swan or something and it gave him such a stunning shock that he'd write a marvelous poem about it.[2]

That intensity of awareness, that ability to look at the familiar and *see* it as if for the first time, sets not only the great poet but also the great reporter apart from the merely competent.

Most of the time we look and do not see. But many people who are drawn to writing sense from childhood that they have a special ability to observe the world, to capture the moment that others overlook, to see "the edges" of things.

Joan Didion says her attention was always drawn to the concrete rather than to the abstract, and in her writing both as a journalist and a novelist she uses biting imagery to convey her views of modern culture. In college, she recalls:

My attention veered inexorably back to the specific, to the tangible, to what was generally considered, by everyone I knew then and for that matter have known since, the peripheral. I would try to contemplate the Hegelian dialectic and would find myself concentrating instead on a flowering pear tree outside my window and the particular way the petals fell on my floor. I would try to read linguistic theory and would find myself wondering instead if the lights were on in the bevatron up the hill. . . . I can no longer tell you whether Milton put the sun or the earth at the center of his universe in "Paradise Lost," the central question of at least one century and a topic about which I wrote 10,000 words that summer, but I can still recall the exact rancidity of the butter in the City of San Francisco's dining car, and the way the tinted windows on the Greyhound bus cast the oil refineries around Carquinez Straits into a grayed and obscurely sinister light. In short, my attention was always on the periphery. . . .[3]

In fact, the "best" journalist has a poet's instinct for minute details. In this sense, the demands imposed on writers of nonfiction—the need to be specific, to use the concrete to trigger an intangible but powerful response—are similar to the demands imposed on poets and novelists.

It is an attempt to order description that will evoke emotion, convey innuendo, imply the imminence of revelation. Feature prose that packs a wallop demands this kind of poetic sensibility. It demands the concrete. It demands brevity that comes from selection, not compression. It demands an awareness that what is left out is just as important as what is put in. In fact, some of the best journalistic description is sometimes just a carefully constructed list. Here is how one writer describes the experience of a suburban family who is being harassed by local teenagers:

> BB pellets, slingshots, broken windows, a burning shoe, stolen trash cans, uprooted wooden flower planters, broken aerials, foreign cars hefted onto lawns, trash fires, tossed raw eggs, broken beer bottles, curses, loud radios, loitering, trees set on fire, fights. And snowballs. Every winter, snowballs.[4]

The following feature, on former model Christie Brinkley just after her much-publicized divorce trial, leans on detail, detail, detail to sketch a vivid portrait:

> Her hair is thick and golden, her skin is tanned but only just. Her teeth are gleaming, her waist is narrow, and she's dressed like the popular girl from your high school: tight red tank top, tight dark jeans, groovy purple sneakers laced up in some complicated unlaced way, and sporty Oakley shades. One wrist is wrapped with an uncomfortable-looking amount of beads and baubles and charms and two leather bands in Rasta colors that demand, STOP GLOBAL WARMING NOW![5]

Capture the Details

A feature writer's list of images, of course, is constrained by facts, and it is always annoying, not to mention unethical,

51

when writers untether their concrete facts and let them soar into the stratosphere of purple prose. But most beginning writers do not even begin to develop the descriptive possibilities of a story. They miss what Didion calls the "shimmer" around the edges of things. To write a good story, you must note those edges: color, texture, smell, sound, quiet, tone of voice, body language, small things lying around.

Say, for instance, you are doing a feature on an all-night diner. You walk in at midnight. One customer, a man, is sitting alone in the back, eating a sandwich.

What is he wearing? Are his clothes pressed or wrinkled? Frayed or new? What kind of shoes does he have on? What brand and color? Expensive or cheap? Is he wearing socks? If so, what color and are they snug or sagging? What is he eating? Does he eat it fast or slow? How does he hold his fork? Is he a crumb-wiper? A chin-dabber? A dribbler? What is his posture: erect, hunched, legs crossed, ankles crossed, shoulders tilted in one direction? Does he seem self-conscious or relaxed, and what is it about the way he sits and moves that conveys this impression? Is he reading? If so, what? Is he on a cell phone? Texting? What color is his hair? Thick or thin? Well-cut or shabby? Is he wearing glasses? What color are the frames? What is the quality of the way he looks at other people in the restaurant: curious, furtive, shameful, eager, indifferent? What is it, specifically, that conveys that quality? What is the shape of his face?

These are a fraction of the questions about this man for which you should have the answers, written in your notes, before you leave the diner. Then you need to turn your attention to the physical description of the diner itself, to the interaction or lack of interaction among people—to the ambiance or "vibes" of the place and its occupants. How does the diner smell? Is there background music? What exactly is playing? If you don't know, ask. Are there other noises? Who else is there? Remember to get specifics: How long—exactly—is the counter and what is it made of? What color is it? What's on the menu?

A certain feeling comes over writers as they gather this kind of careful description. It is like having radar on the top of your head, slowly circling round and round. While going through this process, most writers feel distanced, disengaged from not only the scene but from themselves: they become objective non-participants, neutral, focused in the moment, human computers dedicated to sorting and storing information. This is why it is very important *not* to report on an event in which you are also a participant. If you are going to write about a game, a meeting, a concert, a beach, don't plan to join in the action and just take a few notes along the way. If you're going to report, then report. If you're going to join, then join. The two don't mix. Experienced feature writers know this; novices usually learn the hard way.

When gathering information, it is also very important to *write down everything*. Later, you can decide what to throw out and what to keep. The tendency, unfortunately, is to think: "Oh, I'll remember that he wore wire-framed glasses, and the exact words on his T-shirt. Besides, I probably won't need that kind of stuff anyway." Then you arrive back at the office or home, begin to write, and find yourself searching for that tiny missing detail to flesh out the story, or to illustrate a point. Now *why* did he seem sinister? You're sure it wasn't your imagination, but how can you show it to the readers?

Not only have you wasted time looking through your notes for information that is not there, you may have also lost the opportunity to choose that "perfect" detail to illustrate your story.

Consider, for example, the kind of notes this reporter must have been taking when he visited Major League pitcher Pedro Martinez's home:

> After every game in Queens, he goes home to Cruz, and
> to a wonderland. A winding paved driveway leads to his

53

house, which is about a quarter of a mile from the road. Two waterfalls trickle down a 20-foot-tall formation of rocks. In the distance is a pond big enough for a rowboat. Chipmunks scurry between the shrubs. Bumblebees bounce from tulip to tulip. The sound of birds chirping is so constant that it seems like a piped-in recording on the property, which a landscaper helps Martinez maintain.

Beneath the porte-cochere sits his white Hummer. In the backyard is a swing set that his two children from a previous relationship can use when they visit. Inside, cathedral ceilings and gigantic windows make the home feel airy. And last week, that air was filled with the aroma of sancocho, the traditional Dominican meat soup. One of Martinez's cousins from the Dominican Republic was in the kitchen stirring a large vat of it.[6]

The soothing, mesmerizing, lulling quality of this description—bumblebees and birds, waterfalls and Hummer, cathedral ceilings and sancocho—transports the reader to a lifestyle built on fame, wealth, and dreams fulfilled.

Notice the Nuances

The most difficult things to describe are the intangibles—smells, body language, a certain look in the eye, the sound of a voice. The announcer in Pennsylvania Station (see chapter 3) had a way with words. Here is a careful description of his pronunciation of just two of them.

You really have to be there to appreciate Mr. Simmons' snappy, syncopated "All aboard." He pauses after the train's last destination and takes a breath before leaping on the first "a" in "all," holding it for a while, then lingering on the double l's. He then attacks the first "a" in "aboard," holds the "o" for the longest time and bites the word off at the end: "Haaallll haaboooo-wit!" It packs a wallop, and sometimes sets patrons of the adjacent Nedicks restaurant to running out with napkins flying.[7]

The writer manages to reproduce the sound of every letter in these two words and as shown in chapter 3 conveys them with an assist from great verbs (pauses, leaps, lingers, attacks, holds, bites, packs a wallop). This is the kind of detail to strive for.

Put It All Together

When you are ready to sit down and write, you then have to decide how to put it all together—which description to include, where to put it, and what to leave out. Here are a few observations and suggestions.

Be Highly Selective

Most beginning writers use too much description, thrown about too haphazardly. In the following example, it takes only two sentences to graphically convey several hours of rioting in Miami:

> Demonstrators, outraged at the seizure of Elian Gonzalez by a gun-toting federal SWAT team, shouted, wept, waved flags and signs and—in isolated angrier outbreaks—blocked traffic, threw rocks, overturned bus benches and torched tires and trash bins. Police met them fast and forcefully—some say too forcefully—pumping tear gas canisters into crowds and hauling off dozens in handcuffs.[8]

Whether the action is violent or benign, several hours can be reduced to several sentences through careful selection of detail. Here, a "typical" day for nannies in New York's Riverside Park is handled in three well-chosen sentences:

> The nannies gather at the playground every day to talk of Pampers, prams and Presidential politics while watching the toddlers in their charge ride a myriad of plastic vehicles, swing on the swing set, and "socially interact": drooling on other children, poking fingers in their eyes, pulling hair, throwing a little sand in their faces, falling asleep in their presence and just generally having a fine time. Few of the nannies wear the old starched white uniforms. They are too impractical, taking on the look of a painter's palette after 10 minutes with a toddler.[9]

In each of these disparate instances, the writers pack the activity of several hours into a brief paragraph. To do this, they focus on action: demonstrators torching tires and trash bins, police tossing tear gas into crowds; and in a more pastoral setting, children riding plastic vehicles, drooling, throwing sand. Both rely on long sentences laced with subordinate clauses to convey most of the information. And both, after panning the scene, use the last sentence to focus on one specific image that the writers feel most graphically represents the whole: people in handcuffs; the nannies' practical dressing habits.

Zoom In on an Individual

This is especially helpful if you begin with a panoramic description, as above. Here is how a writer handled the description of Grant Park in Chicago when Senator Barack Obama was elected President of the United States. It begins with an eagle's eye description of the park:

> First by the hundreds, then the thousands, then the tens of thousands, Chicagoans converged on Grant Park to exult in the election to the presidency of a man they adopted as one of their own, Senator Barack Obama of Illinois.
> A huge roar arose about 10 P.M. Central time when CNN, displayed on giant television screens, declared Mr. Obama the projected winner over Senator John McCain, his Republican opponent.
> Wave on wave of cheering followed. "O-bam-a, O-bam-a!"
> In the streets around the park, where an overflow crowd of more than 125,000 spilled, people hugged, long, long embraces. Some cried, others broke into dance.

Then, close-ups of people:

> Rose Mary Day, 62, of Chicago, watched with tears in her eyes. "It's history," she said. "It's elating. I feel the way I did as a young girl when J.F.K. was elected."
> "I can't believe today is the day; I can't believe we're here after working for this for so long," said Karen Davis,

56

46, who volunteered for Mr. Obama's campaign. "It gives me a chill."

LaToya Strom, 26, who arrived on Tuesday morning in hopes of getting a decent vantage point, said she had awoken especially early and grew tearful when she imagined what the day might bring.

Although she did not yet know the result of the day's voting, Ms. Strom, who is African-American, said, "Something has changed by going through this whether you are black or not."[10]

In the following feature about a soup kitchen, a writer showcases five people out of five hundred who came to have lunch one day in March:

Panorama: Some of them simply file in and file out, picking up a bowl of soup and a bagel, eating it quickly, going their way.

Close-up #1: But there is also *the Russian immigrant* in topcoat and fedora, a plaid scarf tucked beneath his long black beard, who eats and then sleeps sitting up in his chair.

Close-up #2: There is *the young woman* with the backpack, dirty feet and dull eyes, who keeps going back for more bread,

Close-up #3: and *the neatly dressed older man* who comes every day at 10 AM to help set up and stays until the linoleum is washed down in late

Panorama: afternoon. Many stop to greet Mrs. Green or Father Frew as though they were the owners of a nice little bistro.

Close-up #4: "Fine meal," said *one man,* shaking the priest's hand, while

Close-up #5: *another* kissed Mrs. Green on one cheek and said, "Now you take care of yourself, O.K.? I'll see you Monday."

Close-up #6: Then the *first man* stood back and sang in a mellow baritone for a minute, "to pay for the meal." When he was finished, everyone applauded. "See, I'm a drunk, but I'm a nice drunk," he said with a smile.[11]

Showcase a Specific Person

This technique is especially useful to help a writer "human-ize" a complex political or social issue. For example, for many years and across several American presidents, the tangled debates over proposed health care reform made it difficult to cover the issues without losing the reader almost instantly. By showcasing a specific person, that person can then symbolize a larger group that is representative of a particular argument or topic of the debate:

> From 10 PM to 6 AM, five nights a week, [Garcia] washes windows, cleans desks and picks up the potato chip bags and used condoms that students leave behind in the library. . . .
>
> When she returns to her mobile home off Southwest Eighth Street just after dawn, she takes the pills she gets through a Jackson clinic. Some are for high blood pressure. One is for the pain in her arms.
>
> For now, there's nothing to be done about a blood clot that formed on her calf and blackened the leg from knee to ankle. She needs an operation. But when the doctor told her it would cost $4,000, she laughed. "Where do you get that kind of money?"
>
> Garcia, who makes $6.70 an hour, has no health insur-ance.[12]

When highlighting one or a few people to represent many, however, it is very important to be fair, to select a person or variety of people who can reflect accurately one aspect of an issue, belief, economic situation, or lifestyle.

When Describing Feelings, Show Don't Tell

Or, as Mark Twain put it, "Don't say the old lady screamed. Bring her on the stage and make her scream." At the University of Wisconsin, the late journalism professor Wilmott Ragsdale used to give his students the following

58

advice about the reporting of emotions (those who heeded it went on to become some of the country's top journalists):

> When a character is said to be afraid, jealous, sexually excited, embarrassed, or hating, the reader or viewer will share the emotion only when enough of the particular *signs* of the emotion are given.
>
> The particular signs, the concrete instances, the facts given us are usually those that we get by way of our senses: things we see, hear, touch, taste, smell. We are given these specifics (symbols) in a sequence. Both the specifics themselves and the order in which we are given them will help determine the feelings that are aroused in us as we read or see.
>
> Hemingway seems to be speaking of this process when he says that he always sought "the real thing, the sequence of motion and fact which made the emotion."
>
> T. S. Eliot seems also to be speaking of this process in his essay on *Hamlet:* ". . . the only way of expressing emotion in art is by finding an 'objective correlative': in other words, a set of objects, a situation, a chain of events which shall be the formula of that particular; such that when the general facts, which must terminate in sensory experience, are given, the emotion is immediately evoked."
>
> Ralph Waldo Emerson in his essay on "nature" also appears to be describing this same process: ". . . Every natural fact is a symbol of some spiritual fact. Every appearance in nature corresponds to some state of the mind, and that state of the mind can only be described by presenting that natural appearance as its picture."
>
> Nearly *every sort of writer chooses specifics and puts them in an order that will cause feelings in the reader.* There are both diffuse, sloppy feelings and precise, concentrated, accurate feelings.
>
> The skill with which the writer chooses the specifics and orders them determines how well he or she can communicate the feeling to the reader.[13]

Don't announce to the reader that the person you are describing is feeling a particular emotion (he felt sad; she felt nostalgic; they were furious), *unless you back it up with a specific example to show this feeling.*

In this profile, the writer peels away the layers of a successful French fashion designer's anxieties through carefully selected detail:

> Elbaz thinks it's a very big deal that he is overweight. Asked what he imagines life would be like if he were thin, he replied, "Amazing," with real conviction. But he isn't very big, just round. . . . His jowls are soft, his eyes are blue and framed by long lashes and large, rectangular glasses, and his sartorial choices—too short pants, cap-toed shoes with no socks, and always a bow tie fashioned from silk or velvet or a length of grosgrain ribbon—give him the appearance of a dreamy, somewhat forlorn French schoolboy. (He is, in fact, forty-seven.) Elbaz worries constantly and openly. . . . In 2004, Irving Penn photographed Elbaz, and the designer proudly sent a print to his mother. When she saw it, she asked her son, "Why do you look sad? And who are you scared of?"[14]

These simple descriptions of body and personal style, and his recollections of the comments from his mother, are the writer's tools used to reveal some of the complexities of personality.

When describing groups of people who can't be interviewed directly, writers must be careful not to paint all people with the same brush. In describing a group of chic young shoppers at an expensive clothing store in a local shopping mall, one beginning writer wrote: "The store was filled with spoiled rich kids using their daddies' credit cards, more out of boredom than anything else."

The problem here is that the writer has committed the crime of overgeneralization. How does she or he know that every customer in the store is rich, spoiled, bored, and using a father's credit card?

Take just one of these blanket assumptions: boredom. As a writer, you can safely use a word like "bored" only if you support that contention with evidence—with specific illustrations of boredom. These may include yawns, tapping fingers, glazed eyes, nail-biting.

And remember that even these acts may not necessarily reflect boredom. A person under stress may bite his nails; a shy person in a public place may seem listless and disinterested in people around her. When you interpret these acts as boredom, you risk losing credibility with the reader. It is better to just describe a few people doing things that reflect the mood of a situation, and let the reader reach into his or her own experiences for interpretation. This approach keeps the writer in the background. It lets the reader respond to the story, rather than to the writer's analysis of the story.

When it comes to emotions, it is unlikely that every person in a given situation is responding or acting in precisely the same way. If you write "all," it probably reflects a critical lack of attention to "each."

Be suspicious of yourself when you perceive an entire group of people as bored, happy, anxious, upset, excited. You may be the one who is feeling that way, or who would feel that way if you were in their situation. The same principle of caution applies when describing an individual. A woman who wipes her brow may be nervous, or just hot. A man who is laughing may be happy, or simply obsequious.

In the following description of the one-year anniversary memorial service for those who died during the 2001 attack at the World Trade Center in Manhattan, the writer does not say what the people at the memorial were feeling, only what they were doing. But the choice of description, if it is apt, will *evoke* some feelings in you, the reader.

> They followed one another down, down into a seven-story hole in Lower Manhattan yesterday, thousands of them, filling with their sorrow the space where their husbands and wives, mothers and fathers, sisters and brothers, sons and daughters, had died a year ago to the day.

61

Some left cut flowers on the hard earth; some left photographs; some left whispered words.

They lingered for a long while; a few even collected stones. And then the people who have become known as the "family members"—as though they belonged to one international family—trudged back to level ground, to the living.[15]

These simple actions are universally understood to reflect the emotions of respect and grief. The use of these shared cultural signs helps arouse similar emotions in the reader.

Or consider this description of a photograph of a young man about to face tragedy.

In only one of the pictures is Bernie alone. He is standing in a sunlit field of tall grass and flowers. He has on jeans and no shirt. His body is casually proud and muscular. He looks wistful and mellow, as if he knows a secret that would take too much effort to share. It's the kind of picture a girlfriend would have enlarged to put on her bulletin board.

Bernie asked his sister Becky to take the photograph. She used the last frame on the roll. It is the last shot made of Bernie when he could stand alone.[16]

Soon after the picture was taken, swimming champion Bernie Jorn of Baltimore, Maryland, broke his neck in a diving accident at the age of seventeen and became a quadriplegic. The reporter who described Bernie's life before and after the accident chose this photograph as an effective vehicle to personalize the tragedy.

Wrap Description around Strong Verbs

Reread chapter 3. Remember that description alone, with no redeeming action, stops the story in its tracks. If you use description with weak or passive verbs, be sure you are doing it *with the intent* to create a special effect.

As in this lead, for example:

It *is* noon in January in the high Arctic. The sun *went* down two months ago and *hasn't been seen* since. It *is* dark and foggy. The wind *blows* at 30 knots off the Arctic Ocean. The wind-chill factor *is* 50 degrees below zero.[17]

This lead itself is "cool," like the land it describes. The stagnant verbs, the stilted sentences, convey a sense of frozen isolation, unchanging terrain. They help to anchor the reader in this dark and lonely place before moving into the feature.

But as a general rule, it is always better to weave description with action. You may not want to do this in every sentence, but it is a good idea to be generous with "action" sentences. This is especially difficult to do when describing what people are wearing. Notice how in this feature on a family reunion, the writer mixes descriptions of clothing with a few specific actions to keep it moving along.

> One of Aunt Rosalene's grandsons, sporting a straw cowboy hat that Willie Nelson himself would envy, *saunters* in with a good-looking girl in shorts. Three sisters from south Florida *wear* matching T-shirts that chronicle the event: "Clements Family Reunion '80." A long-haired college girl that someone says is a Sigma Nu sweetheart *strums* a guitar. Kids in cut-off jeans and football jerseys *scamper* off through the pines to a nearby playground and swimming pool.[18]

These are quiet, almost gentle, sentences. The verbs are unobtrusive. But they make the difference: without their subtle help, the sentences would be lifeless on the page.

EXERCISES

1. What's wrong with the following description? How can it be improved? Rewrite it.

> The popular restaurant on Main Street will open in an hour at 6 PM. The six-person wait staff sits around an empty table and listens to the manager who rattles off the list of evening specials, including a vegetarian lasagna. It's late September and the air is stuffy because the air conditioner is not working at full blast. The staff is hot in their uniform of blue shirts and khaki pants. The average age of the wait staff is 21; all except one are college students who are working part time. The full-time employee, Sam, 26, tall and lanky, is an actor. The manager, Sharon, a

petite red-head who never stops talking, urges the wait staff to "upsell" more by encouraging customers to order mixed drinks and appetizers. She holds a dessert tray with samples of seven different cakes and pies and tells the staff to bring the selection to the table automatically, without asking the customers. The average check in the restaurant is $42 and Sharon suggests that with a little assertiveness the staff can push it to $50, leading to bigger tips, too.

2. How can the description that follows be improved? Rewrite, condensing to one sentence.

Thirty toned and fleshy bodies clad in thirty combinations of exercise attire scatter across the rubberized floor like litter on a windy day. They line the walls, using exercise machines and free weights. Some stand to bend, some sit to stretch, some lie on their sides and lift their legs to one-two routines, some do sit-ups, or cool down. Others mill about and schmooze. The air hangs, thick with sweat. Television monitors glare over the treadmills, with picture but no sound.

3. Go to a public place and write down careful descriptions of everything you see, hear, sense, and smell. Be a passive observer. Do not interview. Do not participate. Be sure to choose a place where you can spend an hour or two (but avoid libraries or other quiet places). Then write a 500-word story about the place, capturing its ambiance through appropriate (not excessive) detail. What major problems do you encounter in your writing? What details did you miss? Be sure to use good verbs to keep it moving.

Some examples of places you might go:

- an airport or bus or train station
- a gym
- a sporting event
- a shopping mall
- a popular museum

- a park
- a fast-food restaurant
- a town hall or city council meeting

NOTES

[1] *Writers at Work: The Paris Review Interviews*, George Plimpton, Ed., Fourth Series (New York: Viking Press, 1976), p. 236.

[2] Op. cit.

[3] Joan Didion, *The New York Times Book Review*, December 5, 1976.

[4] Stephen Braun, *Baltimore News American*, January 13, 1980.

[5] Amy Larocca, *New York* magazine, August 17, 2008.

[6] Juliet Macur, *The New York Times*, May 9, 2006.

[7] William Geist, *The New York Times*, January 5, 1985.

[8] Sandra Marquez Garcia, Tyler Bridges, and Curtis Morgan, *Miami Herald*, April 23, 2000.

[9] William Geist, *The New York Times,* October 17, 1984.

[10] John M. Broder and Monica Davey, *The New York Times*, November 5, 2008.

[11] Anna Quindlen, *The New York Times*, March 5, 1983.

[12] Ana Menendez, *The Miami Herald*, March 1, 2006.

[13] From class notes prepared by Wilmott Ragsdale, former journalism professor, University of Wisconsin and University of Puget Sound (WA). The late Professor Ragsdale was a gifted teacher, mentor, and inspiration to hundreds of writers.

[14] Ariel Levy, *New Yorker*, March 16, 2009.

[15] Dan Barry, *The New York Times,* September 12, 2002.

[16] Greta Tilley, *Greensboro News & Record* (NC), March 30, 1986.

[17] Ken Wells, *Wall Street Journal,* February 7, 1984.

[18] Bib Dart, *Atlanta Journal-Constitution*, August 2, 1980.

Quotes are powerful allies. A good quote should reverberate. It should have resonance. It should set your story on edge. A good quote should reveal the quoted person's beliefs, motives, secrets, whims, hidden agendas, pain, sense of humor, philosophy, erudition, expertise, passion, ignorance, or fatal flaw. If you dislike a person, you can dangle her from the noose of her own words. If you admire someone, you can endear him to the reader through a few well-turned quotes.

But, like description, a little bit goes a long way. Let quotes do the work *only* when you cannot find a better stylistic tool to do it for you.

Use quotes sparingly. Few people are highly quotable, and the best-written profiles contain only a light sprinkling of quotes. Don't lean on quotes. Never quote something when you can paraphrase it better in your own words, such as statistics or basic background information like: "My grandfather was a miller in Sherburne, NY, and he always had a few trotting horses. He owned them, bred them, and raced them in the county fair circuits."

The factual, the obvious, the oblique, and the just plain boring should be condensed and paraphrased by the writer. Remember that quotes are another form of color. Use them with wisdom and discretion to maximize effectiveness.

The Best Kinds of Quotes

In feature writing, good quotes can be put to good use in three powerful ways:

First, they *lend credibility* to the story by providing inside information or opinion.

Second, they make the story feel *immediate.* A good quote moves the reader into the heart of the story. The reporter is no longer the obvious gatekeeper between reader and event. Instead, the reader comes face to face with another person's experiences and beliefs.

And third, with the exception of quotes used to support a statement with an expert opinion, all quotes evoke some *emotion*—bemusement, empathy, sadness, annoyance, humor. That, at least, is the aim. Even the funniest quote is probably not going to tickle every funny bone; even the most poignant comment is not going to send a shiver up every spine. But they should strike home a majority of the time.

Here are 10 ways in which quotes can best be used.

To Praise

Here, a physician comments on a colleague's career as a family doctor:

> "Rod even way back was the ultimate physician," [he] says. . . . "It's just a gift, like a football player who runs fast. He has that gift, a gift of caring and true compassion, all the good qualities, and we all recognized it."[1]

To Convey Loss

This widow is almost inarticulate in her grief, yet the pain of her loss comes through:

> "If he was forgotten, I think I would have felt worse," she said as some of the police officers stooped to kiss her cheek. "I miss him—forget it, I can't explain to you. You try to get on with your life and—forget it, I can't talk about what it's like."[2]

Any sense of loss—whether fleeting or permanent—is usually best conveyed by the person who has gone through the experi-

68

ence. Take, for instance, the rather mundane experience of parents saying good-bye to a child leaving for summer camp. This reporter captures the ambivalence that tugs at many parents' hearts:

> Mr. Mandel, who talks much about the carefree, childless life, recalled clutching his 9-year-old son at the bus and his son finally saying: "Dad, can I please get on the bus now?"
>
> "Half of you," said Mr. Mandel, "wants him to be confident and independent and the other half of you wants him to say 'I can't go, I love you too much.' I just have the feeling all the time like something is missing. . . ."
>
> "He's been gone two weeks and a little more than a day now."[3]

To Express Reaction to Trauma

During a school shooting at Virginia Polytechnic Institute and State University (Virginia Tech) in Blacksburg, 32 people were killed and many others wounded. Afterward, a student who survived shared her new sense of vulnerability:

> "You'll never answer the question why some people were killed and some people weren't," [she] said. "The way you sat. The way you were lying under your desk. The way you got hit. We'll never know." [4]

A 22-year-old burn victim from Rockford, Illinois, who spent nine weeks in the hospital undergoing excruciating therapy and surgery, tells what she has learned from her ordeal:

> I know there's a God and there's a purpose for my being here. And I know I won't go to hell—because I've already been there.[5]

To Convey a Private Opinion about a Public Situation

An FBI agent had this to say about organized crime in Las Vegas:

> "When I'm told there is no organized crime representative in Las Vegas, that's ridiculous on its face. I laugh at

'em. You have to accept those kinds of statements for what they're worth, and they're worth nothing."[6]

To Let People Describe Their Own Work, Hobby, or Lifestyle, Provided They Do It in a Pithy Way

Here's how one man described the bar he owned on the banks of the Rosebud River in Jimtown, Montana:

> "I'm the fifth owner of this joint. The first was a guy named Jim Ellison. That's how the place came to be Jimtown. It isn't a town. I guess you noticed this is the only thing here, this saloon. Isn't it the worst place you ever saw?"[7]

Or who but an experienced farmer can better describe the sinister seductions of heavy farm machinery? While the economic context of this story may change over the years, the end result remains the same:

> "Machinery can be intoxicating. You sit there on top of a huge tractor, rolling across those fields, and you feel like God. It's an amazing feeling, and a real one, and I think some people get so they don't feel complete without it.
>
> "That's one of the reasons they keep buying bigger and bigger tractors, these enormous four-wheel drives, tearing up and down the fields. Tearing up and down. They are incredibly expensive machines; they'll run you $16 an hour in fuel alone, and you can do in one day what used to take you three or four—but then the question arises, are you doing anything useful on the three or four you saved? You buy this gigantic machine with its incredible capability and all of a sudden, you're done.
>
> "And you start thinking, 'My God, if I bought another 600 acres I could do that, too.' So you buy it, and then you find if you only had a bigger machine, you could buy even more. At the end of it, you're doing 2,000 acres on this fantastic Star Wars machinery and you're so far in debt that if anything goes wrong—and I mean if they stop eating soy sauce in Ireland—you lose the whole works, including the place you started with."[8]

During the Feast of St. Francis of Assisi, a reporter interviewed the proud owner of a show elephant named Mignon outside the Cathedral of St. John the Divine in New York

70

shortly before the pachyderm walked down the aisle for her annual blessing:

> "Mignon's feeling good today," said Bob Comerford, whose livestock travels the county and state fair circuit. "She's just acting up to shock people. Minnie's a pro. Yesterday she was in Newport at a church fair giving rides, and tomorrow she goes to Vermont for a hardware store promotion. This elephant has done it all. She's done opera—the triumphal march in *Aida,* she did in Hartford, Cleveland and Salt Lake City. She's been in *Vogue.* She's filmed dozens of commercials. The one where an elephant steps on a Tonka truck? That's Minnie. I can't even remember everything Minnie has stepped on."[9]

To Highlight a Person's Philosophy, from the Insightful to the Insipid

When the late Rose Elizabeth Bird became chief justice of the California Supreme Court, she had this to say about being "first":

> "I've always said that when you're the first of your sex or your race in a position, three things apply to you," she says. "One—you're placed under a microscope. Two—you're allowed no margin for error. And three—the assumption is always made that you achieved your position on something other than merit."[10]

A year before Hurricane Katrina devastated New Orleans, a coastal engineer commented on the city's vulnerability to flooding caused by human-made changes to the natural ecosystem:

> "When you look at the broadest perspective, short-term advantages can be gained by exploiting the environment. But in the long term you're going to pay for it. Just like you can spend three days drinking in New Orleans and it'll be fun. But sooner or later you're going to pay."[11]

"Philosophy" need not be profound or even very pragmatic. A regular at neighborhood yard sales had this to say about her weekend experiences:

> "My philosophy is, when in doubt, buy," said Loretta. "I've often been sorry about what I didn't get, but I've never regretted what I did."

71

A shopping companion added his own yard-sale folk wisdom: "I'll let you in on another rule. You can sell almost anything at a garage sale, but there's three things you can't even GIVE away: Reader's Digest Condensed Books, aluminum Christmas trees, and cracked bowling balls. Everyone hates carting them around as much as you do."[12]

To Show Interaction between People

Dialogue is the stuff of high and low drama, in life as in art. Used carefully, it can lend a theatrical touch to a feature. Here, a writer uses teacher-student dialogue from a class in which stockbrokers are taught to get new clients over the phone:

"Ring, ring," says a broker, pretending he is making a "cold call" to a hot prospect, played by Mr. Good.

"Hello," Mr. Good says, in a tone that would freeze boiling oil.

"Is Mr. Good there?" the broker asks tentatively.

"No, he's not, you simpering wimp!" The class breaks into laughter.

"Is Mr. Good there?" doesn't sound authoritative, Mr. Good explains. "May I speak with Mr. Good, please" is better, he says, making it sound like a command instead of a request. The trick is to raise the pitch of your voice as you say "Good." Then drop it like a bowling ball as you say "Please."[13]

Dialogue can also show a *failure* to communicate. Here, a husband and wife fight over their Christmas tree:

"You want a fake tree," a woman looking at trees at Broadway and 91st Street was saying to her spouse, "you get a fake tree. It's your decision."

"I don't want a fake tree," the spouse said, "but the artificial trees just seem to make a lot more sense."

72

"Then get a fake one," the woman said, and muttered something about serving Spam for Christmas dinner.[14]

To Reveal Personality

Motivations, attitudes, personal concerns and commitments, emotional problems, an indomitable sense of humor—all can ooze through the surface of a good quote.

Sometimes, even a nonanswer and avoidance of the question can serve up a good quote. Former New York Governor Elliott Spitzer, never noted for his humility, was invited by a reporter to respond to those attacking him for his liaisons with prostitutes. His nonanswer:

> "Let me put it this way," Spitzer says with a smile. "I don't want you to think that I don't have an answer to the question, but I also think you'll understand that I'm probably clever enough not to give it to you. Plus, I'd diminish the value of my memoirs."[15]

An inexperienced writer might have not written this down, and gone away disappointed about not getting a quote. An experienced writer spotted its potential.

Here is a quote from a Wisconsin man who bought 35 woodland acres and then learned that hundreds of containers of toxic wastes had been buried under the access road running through his property. When state officials told him they not only expected him to pay for removing the waste, but also expected him to sue the people who had dumped it there originally, the reporter lets him describe his sense of helplessness:

> "All I wanted was a nice quiet place that had a lot of deer and raccoons and things on it so I could take my family there on outings. I'm afraid of what may be out there under that road and how I'm going to pay for cleaning it up. I've never been involved in anything like this before."[16]

Or, in a feature on residents of a state mental hospital, the reporter focuses on one inmate, 20-year-old "Mary," who, the reporter says, "jumps subjects quickly and randomly." To support this contention, the reporter illustrates with a quote:

> "Uhh-mmmm," she makes a sound in her throat, and grins an impish grin. "Excuse me. I was just wondering, are you writing a book?
>
> "I've been writing since I was 10 years old. I want to be a songwriter or a singer or a disc jockey on a radio station or a fashion model or an actress.
>
> "What's your sign?"
>
> Her fingernails are painted red. Manicures are tricky when your hands shake from medication. In places she has as much polish on her skin as on her nails.
>
> "My parents are separated," she says. "My father's an alcoholic. He has his own problems so he doesn't have too much time for me, but I still love him. I sent him a drawing today."[17]

To Highlight the Drama of a Past Event

Someone who was a witness, victim, or participant in an event can often, in his or her own words, convey the moment in a more immediate way. Students at Stuyvesant High School were in their classrooms in Lower Manhattan when two airplanes hit the nearby World Trade Center on September 11, 2001. One student recalled:

> "Our teacher started crying and told us all to continue working. She closed the shades, which really didn't help because you could still see through them.
>
> "The plane hit in the corner and you could see through the building to blue on the other side. The kid next to me screamed and said he saw people jumping. But I didn't believe him."[18]

The understated, matter-of-fact, almost numb tone of this quote is in itself a dramatic juxtaposition to the violence, and only serves to highlight the tragedy seen through the school windows, and the trauma to those teenagers who saw it.

To Support a Statement with an Expert Quote

For the most part, statistics should be used only in paraphrase. But there are exceptions. An article on the problems facing the juvenile justice system makes the point that children who commit crimes often become criminals as adults.

The writer is careful to let an "expert," a criminal court judge, support this assertion with a quote:

> "Fully 90 percent of the people I sentence as adults, people charged with rape or murder or some other horrible crime, have had problems as juvenile offenders," he said. "That is why I say the only way to significantly cut into adult crime is to cut into juvenile crime."[19]

How to Handle Quotes in Copy

Sometimes a quote that seems good when you hear it falls flat when you read it. This can happen when the writer fails to provide enough *context*—the background information or ambiance pertinent to the quote.

You must be sure your quotes are anchored solidly in the story. Even the best of quotes will lay limp on the page unless they are "set up" properly. What precedes and follows the quote is often as important as the quote itself. Quotes must be highlighted properly or they will be lost on the page.

To set up a quote, the writer needs to prepare the reader in the previous sentence or paragraph. Take, for example, the feature on the Maryland man who became a quadriplegic at age 17. First, the writer sums up the small daily experiences that this young man will never have again. The writer, in effect, distills in a few phrases a lifetime of loss:

> He misses the little things most, things that would better define him as Bernie. A certain walk, a certain stance, a gesture, a firm handshake. To give someone the thumbs

75

up sign, to clap at a concert, to reach over and put his arm around a girl.

Then the writer uses *one single quote* to highlight this deprivation:

> "I'll never forget the first time I realized in the hospital I wouldn't be able to hug somebody. A physical therapist was gonna transfer me. I leaned up against her for the transfer and it felt so good to be close to somebody I started crying."[20]

Occasionally, it is more effective to use a quote *followed* by an anchor, as in this story about a woman who requested that her mail orders be sent via UPS since she had a secret crush on the delivery man:

> "He looked liked Kevin Costner in brown," she sighs, recalling their long talks on her doorstep.
> Four years—and hundreds of packages—later, Dave and Lynn are husband and wife.[21]

This pattern—supporting a quote up front or in back with a paraphrase, a description, or a summation—is used all the time by experienced feature writers. As a "lay" reader, you shouldn't notice it. As a professional writer, you must use it.

As a support system it can (and should) be repeated throughout a story. Here is an example of how it works in a story about an airplane that lost its engines when it was hit by a flock of birds, and was piloted to a safe water landing on the Hudson River between New York and New Jersey:

The Setup:	The plane was losing altitude, but it seemed like the pilot still had control. Then a flight attendant dashed down the aisle in search of a fire extinguisher and panic spread.
The Quote:	"Within a minute, everyone knew what was happening. It became real," said Bill Zuhowski, 23, a Long Islander sitting directly behind Kolodjay.
The Setup:	Any thought that the plane might return to LaGuardia for an emergency landing vanished with the voice of pilot Chesley Sullenberger over the public address system.

The Quote:	"The captain just said, 'Brace for impact,'" Kolodjay said. "And that's what we all did. We put our heads down. We got ready."
The Setup:	Some people locked arms. Others prayed.
The Quote:	"I thought we were going to die. I kept thinking to myself, 'I never got to tell my family I love them every day,'" said grandmother Elizabeth McHugh, 64, of Charlotte, N.C.
The Setup:	An eerie silence fell over the cabin as the blue-and-gray jet plunged a final 100 feet.
The Quote:	"I noticed the New York skyline getting closer and closer," said Dave Sanderson, 47, a married father of four who works for Oracle in Charlotte and was here on business.
The Setup:	The plane hit the water and Sanderson, sitting in 15-A, smacked his head on the seat in front of him. He lifted it to see "controlled chaos" unfolding around him.
The Quote:	"People started running up and down aisles. People were yelling and pushing," Sanderson said.[22]

The brief paragraphs and consistent pattern of vivid summaries interspersed with tight quotes draw the reader through to the very last word.

What to Do with Lots of Quotes

If you find yourself face to face with a notebook full of quotes from, say, a luncheon speech, a court proceeding, or a long interview, consider these possible ways of handling them before you just give up and repeat them verbatim in the story, risking an editor's scorn and your reader's boredom.

Use Partial Quotes

Often, you can integrate a few words of direct quotes into copy without breaking the flow. By placing these partial quotes carefully in the story, you can give added emphasis to a scene. Consider this partial quote from a feature about a riot in

San Quentin prison, during which three prison guards and two prisoners were shot or stabbed to death:

> [The warden] remembers with some precision how he told the guard's wife that her husband was dead, and how her daughters came home afterward, not yet knowing, and the wife knelt to give them crackers to eat. "As though she were giving them communion," the warden says.[23]

Sum Up in Your Own Words

This technique can help you distill the essence of pages of notes and hours of time. For example, in this profile of a Muslim leader, the reporter is present when the imam listens to his voice mail, and uses a few quotes from his messages to reflect the daily scope of his responsibilities:

> The answering machine blinks frantically, a portent of endless questions to come. A teenage girl wants to know: is it "halal," or lawful, to eat a Big Mac? Can alcohol be served, a waiter wonders, if it is prohibited by the Koran? Is it wrong to take out a mortgage, young Muslim professionals ask, when Islam frowns on monetary interest?[24]

String a Few Brief Quotes Together for Star Billing

Note how this writer uses three consecutive quotes effectively in her day-in-the-life profile of a traffic officer. In a city where parking illegally may someday classify as an outdoor sport, Officer Butcher's life is filled with the following lines:

> "I'll just be here for a minute."

> "The sign says you can't park here."

> "I'm a good 10 inches from the hydrant."[25]

Thoughts on Altering a Quote

The general rule is: never change a quote. Never take a quote out of context in a way that changes its meaning. For every hard rule on quotes, there tends to be squishy areas of ambiguity, even among the largest news organizations. The goal is to balance fairness with accuracy. (See the end of this chapter for two news organizations' guidelines on quotes.) For example, within limits, it is reasonable to clean up someone's grammar if it seems unfair to the person to retain embarrassing spoken grammatical errors.

However, there are bona fide occasions when it behooves the writer to retain errors of grammar or syntax: to show regional differences in speech, to reflect a foreign accent, to show a lack of education. But to retain these differences in speech patterns demands careful note-taking.

When some visitors from France gave their view of American sports and television, the reporter noticed their tendency to use the modifier "the" in front of English nouns as they would with French nouns. By keeping this speech pattern in the final draft, the reader can almost "hear" the French accent.

> Sometimes they watch television and try to understand it. "We watch the baseball," Mr. Gres said, "and they are with the clubs and the running. And there is the American football and they jump on top of each other and then get off, time after time."
>
> "And on the news programs there is no analysis," Mr. Fiers said, "just the murder, the fire, the accident; the murder, the fire, the accident."
>
> "And so much publicity!" said Mr. Fiers, speaking of advertising. "You are watching the dramatic production and the hero is chasing to help the beautiful woman and all of a sudden there is a man selling the hamburgers."[26]

When a 19-year-old drifter committed suicide in her jail cell in Virginia, a local reporter pieced together as much as she could of the young woman's life. An unmailed letter, found in her cell, is quoted:

> "I don't really care if you or any of my family doesn't keep in touch," the letter said. "When I need y'all, y'all ain't there."

And a family member is also quoted:

> "She weren't given any help when she needed it. . . .
> There was just nothing nobody could do."[27]

Errors of grammar can add to our information about a person's history and lifestyle. In this last example, for instance, one could extrapolate that the teenager came from a rural Southern family with little formal education. One could be wrong; but grammar can be a clue to a person's past.

How to Get Good Quotes:
The 13 Steps to Success

Be judged not by your answers but by your questions.
—Adapted from Voltaire

Be in Good Mental Shape

An interview demands alertness, quick responses, and good instincts. This means your mind and your equipment— whether it is a digital recorder or a pen and notepad—should be in good working order. If you are sluggish in an interview, you will get sluggish quotes. The interview is a formal ritual, like a waltz, and the interviewer must take the lead. Don't go to an interview tired, distracted, or ill-prepared.

Be Punctual

Allow plenty of time to get to the appointment and build in time for unexpected delays. It is better to arrive early, have a cup of coffee, review your notes, and focus on the interview, rather than to dash in at the last minute.

Be Self-Confident

When you arrive, *act confident,* even if you don't feel it. Beginning writers often feel the person being interviewed is doing them a big favor by "granting" the interview. It is true that you, the interviewer, are there to learn; the interviewee is there to reveal and explain. However, remember that this is a two-way street. Something is in it for both of you. People want their names in print, their positions explained, their contributions—great or small—to be understood and appreciated by family, friends, enemies, and posterity. It is understandable to be nervous during an interview—even the most experienced interviewer feels it. But that nervous energy is an ally; it will help keep you on your toes. Also remember that the person being interviewed probably feels nervous too.

Do Your Research

For public figures, access to background information is easy. Start with search engines, online databases, publication indexes, and reputable blogs. (See chapter 8 for more on research tools and techniques.) For local public figures, you might have to do a bit more digging. When you are researching for your interview, be careful about your sources of information. Keep in mind for both public and private people that inaccuracy and downright lies find their way to the Internet and to printed publications. Once erroneous information is cast into cyberspace, it can never be retrieved. Just because you come across the same fact several times online does not mean it is true. It just means that it is viral. Lean most heavily on a range of reliable, objective, edited sources of information for your facts.

Stories on issues require the same kind of advance research as stories on prominent individuals. Know what has already been published. This will make your questions—and the answers to them—more specific.

Features on private persons—the heroic firefighter, the owner of the new clothing store, the parents of quintuplets—

may not be researchable. But you can get any needed background information during the course of the interview, which you can then check later with friends, employers, neighbors, or in pertinent public records.

Have an Angle Going into the Interview

It is always better to approach an interview subject with a specific angle in mind.

a. Instead of: "I would like to talk to you about your career."

It is better to say: "I would like to talk about why your show went off the air even though the ratings were high."

b. Instead of: "I would like to talk to you about your life."

It is better to say: "I would like to hear how your life has changed now that (you're famous, you're a father, etc.)."

Your angle may change during the course of the interview, and that's okay. But you need a handle going in; otherwise your interview is likely to slide all over the place, and so will your story. It is also far less intimidating for the person being interviewed to be told the interview is focused on a narrow aspect of his or her life. Most people find it overwhelming to think of recounting an entire life, or career, in a single interview. They may end up doing that, but don't tell them you expect it.

Ask Good Questions

This means knowing how to ask questions in a way to get good answers. *Don't ask yes-no questions,* because they produce yes-no answers.

a. Avoid: "So is it true you plan to run for state senator in the next election?"

Ask: "What is involved in your decision about whether to run for state senator in the next election?"

The first question begs for a yes-no answer, and then you will need to ask a series of follow-up questions to try and move the person toward a more thoughtful and compelling quote. The second question forces the person to give a more articulate and reflective answer.

   b. Avoid: "Do you feel happy about being told you just won (the Nobel Prize, the lottery, a trip to Hawaii, etc.)?"

   Ask: "How do you feel about being told you just won the Nobel Prize?"

Again, the first question will produce a yes-no answer. And, just as bad, it projects the writer's reaction to a situation onto the interviewee. The writer assumes winning is conducive to happy feelings. In fact, the subject could be feeling a range of other emotions: fear, scorn, anxiety, ambivalence.

Don't be Afraid to Say "I don't understand," or "Could you give me an example?"

People are often oblique and unclear when they talk, which produces oblique and unclear quotes. It is all right to stop someone in the middle of an interview and ask for clarification or an explanation. Be humble. At worst, this will make the interviewee feel superior to you, and may even lead to some condescending remark; this is most often done by people who feel insecure about what they are saying in the first place, so don't take it to heart. It happens to the best of writers.

The point is to get a good quote, not to earn the undying esteem of the person you're interviewing. At best, asking for an example or a simpler explanation will force the interviewee to clarify thoughts that may still be vague in her or his own mind; it will give you better quotes, and you will be able to write a better story.

Ask Follow-Up Questions

Go into the interview with half a dozen questions typed or written out *clearly* and keep that list in front of you. Leave space between questions on the list, so that as the interviewee is answering one question, you can jot down the new questions being triggered by the answers. That way, if you can't get to the follow-up question right away, you can go back to it before the end of the interview. If you don't write it down, you may forget it.

Go from the General to the Specific

It is always best to start with pleasantries at the beginning of an interview and save the killer questions for near the end. Talk about the weather, the interviewee's family pictures on the desk, the view—anything to break the ice and help the interviewee (and yourself) feel comfortable and get some sense of one another before you proceed. Begin gently.

Investigative writer Jessica Mitford suggested that you list your questions in graduated order from kind to cruel. "Kind questions," she explained, "are designed to lull your quarry into a conversational mood."[28]

As you proceed, you can become more specific and aggressive in your questions, if it is called for. Your tactics will depend in large part on your personality—what style you feel comfortable with—and the personality of your subject. As a general rule, it is better not to force a false interview style on yourself: if you are the quiet, persistent type, don't force yourself to bully people into answers; if you are the bullying type, don't pretend to be sweet and patient. You should modify your approach to suit your subject, but if you are not being honest in your own interview style, chances are the interviewee will pick that up and be less than honest in his or her answers. Be professional. Like a good Scout, be prepared.

Don't Shy Away from Embarrassing Questions

Ask the questions your mother told you never to ask (e.g., "How much money do you make?" "Why did you leave your husband?" "How do you feel about sex now that you're 80?"). Save them for near the end, however. The worst that can happen is that the interviewee will refuse to answer, or will kick you out. Usually, however, he or she will answer.

Be a Good Listener

One of the main interviewing faults of beginning writers is that they talk too much. You don't have to impress the interviewees with how smart you are—your questions will do that. If your subject hesitates, or pauses, don't always butt in with a comment, or a new question. Let a little silence fill the room. Most people are uncomfortable with silence in this kind of situation, and will fill it up by talking. Under this kind of pressure, interview subjects have been known to blurt out the most interesting and incriminating comments. Interrupt only to get back on track, or for amplification. To check on your own listening capacities, tape an interview and then play it back, listening for the number of times you interrupted. If it is more than three to four times in a half-hour interview, you may not be giving your interviewees enough slack.

Take Prodigious Notes

This applies even if you are using a digital recorder. Be sure to take notes of physical details: what the person is wearing, the way he leans back in his chair, how she drinks her coffee, how the office or home is decorated. These details, when correlated with what the person is saying at the time, are essential for adding color to a feature story. (See chapter 4 for more on description.)

Even if you prefer to use a recorder, cover yourself by taking notes of the key comments made in the interview. This

85

way, you have some backup in case your recorder breaks down (and every experienced interviewer has at least one such horror story). Also, relying on a recorder tends to deaden your perceptions in an interview: it is like turning on the television and waiting to be entertained. Taking notes helps keep you alert, engaged in the give-and-take of the interview.

Beginning interviewers are often embarrassed about looking down to take notes: it defies the usual social nicety of looking someone in the eye and nodding attentively as the person bares his or her soul. While it may seem awkward to you, it will not seem offensive to the person being interviewed. On the contrary, it is rather disconcerting to see someone taking notes without looking down (How *will* they read that scribble later on?) and even more alarming to be interviewed and see the person *not* taking notes (Is none of what I'm saying worth anything?). So, scribble away. And don't be afraid to ask the person to slow down so you can catch up, or to repeat a particularly compelling comment. While most reporters do not know shorthand, most develop their own shortcuts in notetaking. Develop some for yourself.

A word about recorders. Many people who are not used to being interviewed will freeze when they see a recorder. Be sure to ask if they mind being recorded. Some people, not wanting to offend, will say they don't mind, and will freeze anyway. If you suspect that is happening, turn off the recorder during the interview.

Recorders are particularly useful if you want a legal record. Although written notes are valid in court, nothing beats having the person's own words available for replay. They are also useful when the person being interviewed is a fast talker, is particularly articulate, or is using terminology with which you are not familiar. The downside, however, is that someone—probably you—will have to transcribe the recording, which can take two to three times as long as the interview itself.

End Well

Your last question should be: "Do you have anything to add?" Often, you have overlooked something that is pertinent. Sometimes, the subject is eager to unburden something that you would have no way of knowing about—unless you give him or her carte blanche to talk about it.

Your last statement should be: "I may be calling you with a few follow-up questions, once I've reviewed my notes." This clears the way for future contact: you don't have to feel embarrassed about calling back; and the subject, having been forewarned, won't be surprised to hear from you again. Make sure you get his or her phone number and e-mail address before saying good-bye.

How the Pros Handle Quotes

Most large news-gathering organizations, whether online or in print, have guidelines for how to handle quotes. Here are two examples:

The New York Times Guidelines on Integrity

> **Quotations.** Readers should be able to assume that every word between quotation marks is what the speaker or writer said. *The Times* does not "clean up" quotations. If a subject's grammar or taste is unsuitable, quotation marks should be removed and the awkward passage paraphrased. Unless the writer has detailed notes or a recording, it is usually wise to paraphrase long comments, since they may turn up worded differently on television or in other publications. "Approximate" quotations can undermine readers' trust in *The Times*.
>
> The writer should, of course, omit extraneous syllables like "um" and may judiciously delete false starts. If any further omission is necessary, close the quotation, insert new attribution and begin another quotation. (*The Times* does adjust spelling, punctuation, capitalization and abbreviations within a quotation for consistent style.) Detailed guidance is in the stylebook entry headed "quotations." In every case, writer and editor must both be satisfied that the intent of the subject has been preserved.[29]

Quotations should always be the exact words that someone spoke, with the exception of corrections in the type of errors, as of grammar and syntax, that often occur unnoticed when someone is speaking but are embarrassing in print. In most cases, the grammar of people for whom English is a second language should be corrected as well. Spoken hesitancies such as um and ah should usually be omitted.

Parentheses within quotations are almost never appropriate and can almost always be avoided. Quotations are used to enliven and emphasize elements of a story, and internal explanations will often bog them down. If many parenthetical explanations are needed, the quote probably wasn't set up properly or wasn't a good quote to start with.

Avoid ellipses within quotations. While reporters often use ellipses in an attempt to remove extraneous elements, to readers they simply signal that we have altered the quotation and raise concerns that we may have changed its meaning in the process. Simply put: ellipses raise issues of credibility. We will, however, use ellipses to remove profanity from quotations.

In cases where we conduct an interview through a translator, we should identify quotes received in that manner ("said through a translator"), as a signal to the reader that there are limits on our ability to attest to the accuracy of the information. In cases where the reporter does the translation, no special designation is necessary, unless the fact that the interviewee spoke in a foreign language is material to the story.[30]

EXERCISES

1. Choose a feature that contains six or more quotes. After reading it carefully, answer the following questions:

   a. What purpose does each quote serve (i.e., does the quote praise, convey loss, etc.)?

   b. In what way does each quote lend credence to the story?

   c. In what way does each quote make the story feel more immediate?

   d. What emotion is evoked by each quote?

2. Using the quotes from the first exercise, analyze the techniques the author applied in the feature, using these questions:

   a. Are the quotes grammatically correct? If not, should they be corrected? Why or why not?

   b. Did the writer ask good, specific questions to get these quotes? Why or why not? Use one quote to illustrate your answer.

   c. How would you improve the quotes in the article you have chosen?

   d. What additional quotes would you suggest the writer get?

   e. What quotes would you take out?

3. Interview a person about his or her job, hobbies, or some other specific personal subject. Be sure to stretch yourself when you select whom to interview. Do not select friends or family members. Choose someone you do not know, in a field that you would like to learn more about. It is the best way to develop your skills. Here are examples of people interviewed by students in a feature writing class, which you can adapt for your community.

   • a marathon runner
   • the owner of a tattoo parlor
   • a fortune teller
   • the owner of a bakery
   • a well-known local journalist
   • a professional videographer
   • a soup kitchen volunteer
   • a popular blogger

   Now write a profile based on the interview. Keep it short—fewer than 750 words. Be careful not to over quote in the profile.

   a. What problems did you encounter in trying to write up this profile? Do you have too many quotes? Are they specific enough? What follow-up questions should you ask to beef up your story?

b. Do a follow-up interview based on the problems you encountered your first time around, and rewrite.

4. Select an interviewer who is known for effective interview tactics. (You can consider, among others, Oriana Fallaci, Lawrence Grobel, John Mcphee, Jessica Mitford, and Deborah Solomon.) Read two of the author's published interviews, then write a 200-word analysis of each, describing a few of the techniques you found most effective. Be prepared to discuss them and back them up with examples.

NOTES

[1] Greta Tilley, *Greensboro News & Record* (NC), October 5, 1986.

[2] Anna Quindlen, *The New York Times*, May 18, 1983.

[3] Neil Cunningham, *Daily Star* (NY), June 18, 1987.

[4] Karen Ayres, *Dallas Morning News*, April 24, 2007.

[5] William Geist, *The New York Times*, July 17, 1985.

[6] Ken Miller, *Reno Gazette Journal* (NV), July 14, 1985.

[7] Jules Loh, *Associated Press*, May 10, 1977.

[8] John Camp, *St. Paul Pioneer Press Dispatch* (MN), May 12, 1985.

[9] Guy Trebay, *Village Voice*, October 15, 1985.

[10] Cynthia Gorney, *Washington Post*, April 8, 1986.

[11] Joel K. Bourne, Jr., *National Geographic*, October 2004.

[12] Jan Hoffman, *Village Voice*, January 27, 1982.

[13] John Andrew, *Wall Street Journal*, March 9, 1984.

[14] William Geist, *The New York Times*, December 19, 1984.

[15] David Margolick, *Vanity Fair*, January 2008.

[16] Nathaniel Sheppard, Jr., *The New York Times*, May 25, 1981.

[17] Greta Tilley, *Greensboro News & Record* (NC), May 2, 1984.

[18] Terri Brooks, *Witness To War* Web Project, Sponsored by The New York Foundation for the Arts, 2002.

[19] Raad Cawthon, *Atlanta Journal-Constitution*, February 22, 1987.

[20] Greta Tilley, *Greensboro News and Herald* (NC), March 30, 1986.

[21] Robert Frank, from *Floating Off the Page: The Best Stories from* The Wall Street Journal*'s Middle Column* (New York: Simon & Shuster, 2002).

[22] Jonathan Lemire, Edgar Sandoval, and Tracy Connor, *New York Daily News*, January 16, 2009.

[23] Cynthia Gorney, *Washington Post*, January 6, 1986.

[24] Andrea Elliott, *The New York Times*, March 5, 2006.

[25] Anna Quindlen, *The New York Times*, April 9, 1983.

[26] William Geist, *The New York Times,* April 20, 1985.

[27] Stacy Burling, *Virginian—Pilot,* April 30, 1981.

[28] Jessica Mitford, *Poison Penmanship: The Gentle Art of Muckraking*, Introduction (New York: Random House, 2011).

[29] The New York Times Company, *Guidelines on Integrity,* Retrieved April 22, 2010, http://www.nytco.com/company/business_units/integrity.html

[30] From *The* San Jose Mercury News *Ethics Policy,* Retrieved April 22, 2010. http://www.mercurynews.com/ethics-policy

Chapter

6

Even the simplest feature has several layers. Beneath the factual "denoted message" of the story lies a series of "connoted messages," which are based on your prejudices, sympathies, education, sense of humor, erudition, and limitations. These connoted messages are implicit in the story.

They constitute your *voice*—active, aggressive, woven into the very fabric of your nonfiction.

Finding Your Voice

In previous chapters, you have seen how the lead, the verb, the description, or the quote can convey a subliminal message that is intended to evoke responses, conscious or subconscious, to your story. However, a single stylistic technique alone does not always give you voice. Your overall success at finding the voice for your story depends ultimately on the way you blend all of the ingredients of your story. It depends on your ability to massage language to suit your needs. Take this story about a homeless 65-year-old woman:

> "I have suffered, oh, no one knows what I have suffered," moaned Sally, holding her head with a gesture that would have brought Sarah Bernhardt to her knees.
>
> Sally says she has been beaten, robbed, mugged and stabbed. She also once swallowed a cockroach, an experience of unrelieved horror, except that a priest had enough presence of mind to give her a long slug of wine to wipe out the taste. Sally is not an alcoholic, but she confides with an air of candor that would do Mary Pickford proud, "I do like apricot brandy. . . ."

> According to Sally, What She Has Suffered all started when her father's brother told him there was gold in the streets of America. "Like a fool, he believed it," she said.[1]

The author has found several ways to reveal her own attitude toward Sally. Comparison with melodramatic actress Sarah Bernhardt and the eternally innocent Mary Pickford (once known as America's Sweetheart) implies that Sally might be exaggerating, but she puts on a good show and is both touching and likeable.

The true horrors—that she was beaten, robbed, mugged, stabbed—are given short shrift, as if the author does not quite believe them. Instead, the author lingers on the cockroach story, describes it as the real "experience of unrelieved horror," and makes sure we learn of Sally's happy ending to that incident. Even Sally's obsessive lament in life—"What She Has Suffered"—becomes like a headline on a Broadway marquee by the simple device of capitalizing the words.

The author's voice, heard through the use of all the above techniques, tells us to be fond of Sally but to not take her too seriously. The author's skill with language makes us smile down on Sally with comfortable condescension.

Or take the following story. On the surface, this is a description of an annual agricultural fair in Massachusetts. The writer is describing two booths at the fair: one run by a group that is opposed to legal abortions, and, across the aisle, another run by a cosmetic company:

> "When do you decide to throw a baby out?" a woman asks the crowd. "This is human life we're talking about." She wore her moral vigilance under a lightly frosted pixie cut, and the Mary Kay Cosmetics representative across the aisle would like to do something about both. Her displeasure shows when the antiabortion harangues interrupt a client consultation. Lipstick cocked at the face of a

milky housewife, she presses her eyes tight and steeples her brows, pausing until the worst is over.

"Abortion . . ."

"I think this is your . . ."

"is a crime . . ."

"color. Let me show you the . . ."

"against nature."

"polish to match."

Over the course of a week at the large fairgrounds, an hour and a half north of Boston, there will be shearing, exhibitions of pulling horses and donkeys, public milking contests, beauty contests for cows and for women, fiddling duels, and greased-pole climbing.[2]

Under the "facts," the author has taken pains to ridicule in several effective ways the woman who is against legal abortion:

- He trivializes her beliefs by implying they are something she wears on the surface, a mere cosmetic gloss, like her "lightly frosted pixie cut."

- He juxtaposes her commentary with makeup advice. By focusing equally on abortion issues and makeup advice, he puts them on the same plane.

- He attributes to the cosmetic saleswoman negative reactions that the writer himself clearly feels ("pausing until the worst is over"), and he describes in detail her pained expression ("she presses her eyes tight and steeples her brows").

- He then moves on to the other events at the fair—"public milking contests, beauty contests for cows and for women." By juxtaposing "beauty contests for cows and for women," he again brings two disparate events down to one common plane, and so mocks Miss America–type contests. He also leaves the impression that this anti-abortionist is just part of the smorgasbord of fun.

The author has arranged his facts and observations to establish voice. By putting two disparate conversations side by side, he conveys his own point of view to the reader.

The Power of Voice

Before we ponder whether or not it is "fair" for writers to include their point of view in a feature, consider a third example. On the surface, it, too, is a straightforward story about a benefit for the Municipal Art Society, with the late Jacqueline Kennedy Onassis as one of the organizers:

She has become the society's lure, the presence the press always reports. She co-chaired its dinner in a tent at the Isamu Noguchi Garden Museum in Long Island City, Queens. The evening was instructive. . . .

As usual, she was the cynosure of all eyes. "The museum is so fresh, so real, so marvelous," she told Mr. [Philip] Johnson. They are dear friends. They agreed that the naked gray tent hung with nothing but Noguchi lamps was spectacular.

Around them, guests craned to get a look. Waiters hovered. A tycoon whom Mr. Johnson knew came by and wangled an introduction. Afterward, she took out her glasses to read the program. She wore black pants and a beaded gunmetal satin jacket. Her enormous earrings were rhinestone. Her bracelet was diamonds.

A breeze set the Noguchi lamps to swaying. Mr. Johnson was entranced. Mrs. Onassis was entranced. Mr. Noguchi looked up approvingly. Miss DeCuevas and Mr. Walton were deep in conversation. Miss Graham hadn't a clue. . . .

The Japanese Ambassador and his wife joined her table. He was transfixed. She pulled out a cigarette, lighted it and one of her giant earrings fell off.

She pushed back her chair. Mr. Johnson pushed back his chair. He crawled around and finally found it in pieces. "Somebody would think you dropped it to spice up the party," he said.

Mrs. Onassis studied her broken earring. Waiters studied her studying. The Japanese Ambassador looked confused. It was explained to him that New York parties were so noisy talk was impossible. He may not have heard. . . .

Mrs. Onassis smiled. Mr. Johnson stared at bits of carrot and gravy congealing on his plate. The speaker droned on, pronouncing city officials "more interesting than others in the world—of course I don't know Paris" and slipped the Statue of Liberty into his finale.

Others spoke. Dessert arrived. Pols worked the room. But the photographers massed to shoot Mrs. Onassis again and again. And at long last, she got up, walked among the tables and delivered her tribute and the society's medal to Mr. Noguchi.

Another must-attend gathering was history. And on her way out, strangers reached out to touch her and tell her how wonderful she had been.[3]

Just under the skin of this story, the author is delivering her jabs. Repeated use of short sentences and paragraphs gives a stilted, artificial feeling to the event. The people seem to move like mannequins: they arrive; they smile; they wave; they push back their chairs; they stare at their jewelry and food and each other. The few quotes are trivial, implying that the speakers are trivial. Because of the writing style, it appears to be a story about disconnection and disengagement, high on style, low on substance.

Is it fair? Your response to the writing in each of the three above examples depends on your feelings about each subject: if you are working for the rights of the homeless, if you are against legal abortion, if you are a fan of Jackie Onassis—you might be annoyed or even angry.

If, on the other hand, you have little sympathy for the poor and displaced, if you support the right to legal abortion, if you get a kick out of ribbing the rich and famous—then these stories might make you smile.

Whatever your response, remember that the feature is intrinsically subjective, not objective. This makes it radically different from the traditional balanced news story, in which different sides are presented in a neutral way, and the opinions and reactions of the author are subordinate to the news itself. In theory, a news reporter should not let his or her personal views influence how the story is written.

97

The feature writer has no such mandate. The feature is not obligated to present all points of view. It is not obligated to be evenhanded. In fact, the most successful feature writers in the last half of the twentieth century (the era that launched many of today's feature techniques) were and are, in many cases, the most opinionated: A. J. Liebling, Tom Wolfe, Joan Didion, John McPhee, Lillian Ross, Hunter Thompson, and Norman Mailer. While they may seldom use the personal pronoun "I" in their nonfiction writing, each writer's voice lies just below the surface of the story, molding it to fit his or her interpretation of events.

This is not to say that the feature writer should not tell the truth: as with straight news, quotes must be accurate and not twisted out of context; description must describe reality, not fantasy; and the writer has an obligation to reflect with some degree of precision the scenario, the personality, or the controversy at hand. But, given all that, the writer has enormous scope to shape the story to reflect his or her personal view of the world.

In this sense, the feature writer is manipulative and controlling. The characteristics that psychoanalysts tell us are harmful to personal relationships work to our advantage when we commit the act of writing. As Joan Didion says:

> In many ways writing is the act of saying I—of imposing oneself upon other people, of saying listen to me, see it my way, change your mind. It's an aggressive, even a hostile act. You can disguise its aggressiveness all you want with veils of subordinate clauses and qualifiers and tentative subjunctives, with ellipses and evasions—with the whole manner of intimating rather than claiming, of alluding rather than stating—but there's no getting around the fact that setting words on paper is the tactic of a secret bully, an invasion, an imposition of the writer's sensibility on the reader's most private space.[4]

With printed page or cyberspace as a shield between them and their projected opinions, writers can bully, ridicule, praise, or pity. But your point of view must have a ring of truth. "The most essential gift for a good writer is a built-in, shock-proof shit detector. This is the writer's radar and all great writers have had it," said Ernest Hemingway, who began his career as a newspaper reporter.[5]

Younger feature writers often produce copy known for its bite, its edge, and its rather merciless gaze on all that is unfair, unjust, immoral, and just plain stupid in the world.

Older feature writers (say, over 35) who stay in nonfiction writing (some move into fiction, some become editors, some educators) and who have retained a purity of vision (many, alas, lose it along the way) have a shot at becoming great writers. Their bite may be more subtle, but with the weight of years it will be deeper. "You develop a consciousness as you grow older which enables you to write about anything, in effect, and write about it well," said Norman Mailer. "That is, provided you keep your consciousness in shape and don't relax into the flabby styles of thought which surround one everywhere."[6] Their good instincts are reinforced by the extra years of just plain living through the complexities of their own personal experiences. And their prose improves with all that practice.

Tom Wolfe is one writer, for instance, who improved with age. His early work in the 1960s like *The Electric Kool-Aid Acid Test*—outrageous for its day in both style and content— charted a new terrain of possibility for nonfiction. Many of today's students say they find it hyperbolic and egocentric and complain that the style interferes with the substance. In his later work, the glare was polished to a deeper sheen. In *The Right Stuff,* for instance (his book about the early days of the U.S. space program), his voice became more forgiving of human foible, without losing its ability to zap and tweak the ludicrous, the inane, the ritualistic and banal.

Establishing Your Point of View

But with this kind of freedom to intrude upon your story comes a responsibility to be aware of the point of view you wish to convey. When you sit down to write, you should already know how you feel about the subject at hand. If not, then you should be aware that you are still sliding around in search of a point of view, and when you find it during the course of writing, you may need to alter parts of the story to fit it, or show clearly within the story itself how or why your point of view has changed. When writing, ask yourself: How do I feel? Why do I feel that way? Is it justified, or should I be suspicious of my reaction? How am I going to convey my point of view in my story? Can I justify this reaction, without getting defensive, if called upon to do so by my editor, my reader, or the people in the story? Am I willing to reevaluate my point of view?

The worst thing a writer can do is to shift his or her point of view in a story without due warning. This befuddles the reader, who first feels led in one direction, then another direction, and finally astray. Whatever ambiguities you feel when writing a story (and there will always be some), they must be sorted out in your own mind. And if expressed in the story, they must be handled clearly and carefully, so the reader has clear signposts along the way. Otherwise, the reader comes to the inevitable conclusion that the writer is incompetent at best, an idiot at worse.

Losing Your Way

What happens when a writer loses his or her voice? Take this example.

Dawn Langley Simmons was a transsexual (man into woman) who shocked Charleston, South Carolina, with both

100

her sex change operation and then her interracial marriage. In the lead to a story, the author tells us that Ms. Simmons is now divorced, and has subsequently become engaged to another man—a felon convicted of committing three murders and a rape, among other crimes.

The author at first seems sympathetic: Ms. Simmons, while quite a character, is made to sound feisty and strong, bright and credible, a person who has overcome enormous odds to find happiness.

The author carefully catalogs Ms. Simmons's woes: illegitimate, a genital deformity, rejected by "well-bred" families. Her first husband robbed her, trading "her Chippendale desks for $10 bills." She plunged into poverty, went on welfare, reverted from successful biographer to a failed writer.

Still empathetic, the author points out:

> She was a more successful man than woman, almost as though she defined woman as victim and proceeded to fit the definition. As a woman she lost the fortune the man had inherited from a distant relative on his mother's side. As a man, Gordon was a prolific and successful author; as a woman, Dawn struggled.

But, midway through the article, the point of view shifts, and the article becomes one of ridicule. It turns out that Ms. Simmons is probably not divorced from her first husband; she insists she gave birth to a girl whom she calls her daughter, but she won't produce a birth certificate; she is probably not engaged to her rapist boyfriend and when she visits him in prison, he spends most of their time together ignoring her "and she ignores the fact that she is ignored."

She now lives in squalor—described in detail by the author—in upstate New York. Her daughter, 13, sleeps in filth.

> In the child's room are no lights. . . . A torn-open mattress disgorging its stuffings, naked of sheets. An awful stench of animal droppings. Upon the bed are three large dogs. . . . On the floor are newspapers soaked with the leavings of dogs.

Then, after this distasteful information, the author does another about-face. Although Ms. Simmons now is made to

101

seem like a loser and a liar, not to mention a lousy house-keeper, the author suddenly ends on a note of praise.

> Inside this strangely draped figure, is a lovely delicacy of mind. And there is delicacy at [Ms. Simmons's] home, too, a home that lacks enough electricity, heat, and even food, a squalid place, really, but a place that has a dignity about it, the same dignity that Dawn Simmons retains in spite of her misfortunes. She manages always to be broke but not poor. In the most unnatural life she has made for herself, with its postures, excesses and contradictions, one strange fact seems to ring the most true: She is a Lady.

The reader is left not only at a loss about what is really going on here, but also with feelings of frustration (or ridicule, depending on your proclivity) aimed at the author due to the mixed messages created by a wavering point of view. Where is the delicacy of mind in this woman who loves a rapist who ignores her? Where is the dignity in the squalor? What is lady-like about being a victim? Did we miss something here?

The author missed something—in fact, quite a few things. It seems like the author could not take the story in hand, or come to terms with any of the ambiguities of the subject and then convey them in a way that didn't make the reader feel jerked about like a marionette. Some of the problems in this story could have been solved if the author had effectively *shown*—through description, anecdotes, or quotes—the dignity, the delicacy of mind, the "ladylike" qualities of the subject, instead of just *telling* the readers they are there, somewhere—if indeed they are. The author didn't take advantage of the linguistic tools that were available.[7]

Combining Voice and Language

How do you keep your words—and your story—firmly under your control? It is not easy. The "rules" of language are shifting and malleable rules, made to be bent or broken, rules that we mold and transform through use, through neglect, through serendipity. It is now possible, for example, to split an infinitive, or end a sentence with a preposition, and still be considered literate. By language we mean both basic grammar

> *"All I know about grammar is its infinite power."*
> *—Joan Didion*

and syntax—the way words are put together in a sentence, the way the sentence is placed in the paragraph, the paragraph in the story. Didion comments on the difficulties and dynamics of language when she says:

> All I know about grammar is its infinite power. To shift the structure of a sentence alters the meaning of that sentence, as definitely and inflexibly as the position of a camera alters the meaning of the object photographed. Many people know about camera angles now, but not so many know about sentences. The arrangement of the words matters, and the arrangement you want can be found in the picture in your mind. The picture dictates the arrangement. The picture dictates whether this will be a sentence with or without clauses, a sentence that ends hard or a dying-fall sentence, long or short, active or passive. The picture tells you how to arrange the words and the arrangement of the words tells you, or tells me, what's going on in the picture.[8]

Didion's "pictures in your mind" is your voice, your point of view, which will determine how you shape your story. Take this simple sentence: I love only you. Then note how the meaning changes when one word—"only"—is rearranged:

- I only love you.
- I love you only.
- Only I love you.

Every minor change in a sentence carries with it the potential for shifts of meaning, slight or dramatic. Watch for them. Watch out for them.

Here are a few guidelines concerning voice and language.

Aim to Write One Sentence You Love in Every Story

Here are a few good tries:

- On urban litterbugs: "Some of them crumple their litter and drop it stealthily, others do it as an act of defiance,

103

while still others toss it as innocently as a flower girl tosses rose petals at a wedding."[9]

- On the furnishings in a hospital lounge: "The decor is tight budget. Furniture is covered in vinyl and burns from cigarettes that missed the plastic ashtrays. Draperies sometimes sag as if they have seen too much."[10]

- On a rodeo in Wyoming: "It was sunny in Cheyenne, and fat clouds whitened a hard, large sky."[11]

It takes work to have fun with language. But with practice, these kinds of sentences will come more often.

Be on the Lookout for Fresh Metaphors or Similes

In a metaphor, a word or phrase figuratively represents something else. Often this involves personification, in which an inanimate object is given human qualities. An excellent example appears above where "Draperies sometimes sag as if they have seen too much."

In a simile, one thing or person is compared with someone or something else, as in: "There are those who would compare learning to drive in Manhattan with learning to swim in the killer-whale tank at Sea World."[12]

But watch out! With overuse, metaphors and similes degenerate into shopworn clichés, throwaway words, and faded phrases. There are hundred of tattered clichés, all to be avoided like the plague, such as: nick of time, smell a rat, white as a sheet, work like a horse, head over heels, cold as ice, blanket of snow, clean as a whistle, busy as a bee, pearls of wisdom, and, of course, avoid like the plague.

Be on the lookout for fresh ways of phrasing:

- As busy as a moth in a mitten.

- As forlorn as a melting snowman.

- As cool as the other side of a pillow.[13]

John McPhee, a master of the apt analogy, writes of a Georgia man who has a voice as "soft as sphagnum." (This example has the added attraction of onomatopoeia: using words that reproduce the sound of the thing you are describing.) Other McPheeisms include: A woman carries a dead turtle by the tail, "like a heavy suitcase with a broken strap." And the governor's mansion is "a million-dollar neo-Palladian Xanadu, formal as a wedding cake."

Here is how he describes a crane operator as his machine bulldozes the bends in Georgia's Ogeechee River:

> With his levers, his cables, his bucket, and hook, he handled his mats and his tank and his hunks of the riverbed *as if he were dribbling a basketball through his legs and behind his back.* He was deft. He was world class. . . . He was much aware that he was being watched, and now he reached around behind him, grabbed the [tree] stump in his bucket, and *ripped it out of the earth like a molar.* He set it at Carol's feet.[14]

Beneath the careful, solid, and apparently disinterested prose, McPhee's voice rings out.

Prefer Understatement to Overstatement

Hyperbole may work in some cases, but unless you feel comfortable (and safe) following the route of exaggeration, it is better to whisper than to shout.

Three weeks after the Chernobyl nuclear accident in Russia, when the people of adjacent Poland were still understandably worried about the radioactive cloud overhead, a writer used this lead in a story about how the country was coping:

> The Polish authorities, eager to dispel lingering fears about the effects of the Soviet nuclear reactor disaster, are finding that rumor and suspicion have longer half-lives than radioactive iodine.[15]

Since the half-life of radioactive iodine is, in fact, quite a bit longer than three weeks, the lead rings a sour note—especially when the rumors are gone and the half-life ticks on.

Experienced writers know that the best way to convey true horror is to describe it without comment, as John Hersey did in writing about Hiroshima on August 6, 1945, the day the first atom bomb fell.

In conveying the facts of this cruel and brutal event, Hersey chose not to berate the reader with hyperbole. Instead, he quietly described the lives of six ordinary people on that extraordinary day.

One of them was Mr. Tanimoto, a minister. Through his eyes, we see the suffering:

> Mr. Tanimoto, fearful for his family and church, at first ran toward them by the shortest route, along Koi Highway. He was the only person making his way into the city; he met hundreds and hundreds who were fleeing, and every one of them seemed to be hurt in some way. The eyebrows of some were burned off and skin hung from their faces and hands. Others, because of pain, held their arms up as if carrying something in both hands. Some were vomiting as they walked. Many were naked or in shreds of clothing. On some undressed bodies, the burns had made patterns—of undershirt straps and suspenders and, on the skin of some women (since white repelled the heat from the bomb and dark clothes absorbed it and conducted it to the skin), the shapes of flowers they had on their kimonos. Many, although injured themselves, supported relatives who were worse off. Almost all had their heads bowed, looked straight ahead, were silent, and showed no expression whatever.

Another witness was Dr. Sasaki:

> There were so many that [Dr. Sasaki] began to pass up the lightly wounded; he decided that all he could hope to do was to stop people from bleeding to death. Before long, patients lay and crouched on the floors of the wards and the laboratories and all the other rooms, and in the corridors, and on the stairs, and in the front hall, and under the porte-cochere, and on the stone front steps, and

in the driveway and courtyard, and for blocks each way in the streets outside. Wounded people supported maimed people; disfigured families leaned together. Many people were vomiting. A tremendous number of schoolgirls—some of those who had been taken from their classrooms to work outdoors, clearing fire lanes— crept into the hospital. In a city of two hundred and forty-five thousand, nearly a hundred thousand people had been killed or doomed at one blow; a hundred thousand more were hurt.[16]

Hersey's "voice" is here, but he is not shouting. His voice is not colorless, but, rather, relentless: it repels, yet mesmerizes; it is awful, yet compelling. A voice that seems disengaged, almost stunned in the telling, much like the survivors themselves.

Let the Language Reflect the Subject Matter Whenever Possible

If you do this well, you can bring the reader closer to the story and make him or her feel "inside" the subject. If you flub it, so that your attempt at imitation seems only cute or quaint, then you will distance the reader, who will get caught up in your linguistic antics rather than in the story itself.

In a story about a bar in rural Georgia, one writer chose a few colloquialisms to entice the reader:

Patrons of the art of rhymes and rhythms drive over from Shellman's Bluff and St. Simons and Midway and Brunswick to hear him sing and to handle a few long-necked bottles of Bud. It ain't easy to find his place.[17]

Sometimes a quote provides the best and easiest forum for highlighting speech patterns. When an old man in the rural Midwest accidentally killed his own dog, the reporter let him describe it in his own inimitable way:

"I killed him last Friday," Pete says. "Ran over him with my car. I had him out for his run and he ran right in front of me.

"Two yips and he was a goner."[18]

At its best (and you have to be at your best to do it) you can use not only words but also the way the sentences are laid out on the page to reflect the subject itself. Michael Herr did this when writing about his experiences during the Vietnam War. He tried to write *inside* the rage, the exhaustion, the obscenities, the fascination with death of many of the young soldiers involved in jungle combat, as in this paragraph about coming under attack:

> Pucker and submit, it's the ground. Under Fire would take you out of your head and your body, too, the space you'd seen a second ago between subject and object wasn't there any more, it banged shut in a fast wash of adrenaline. Amazing, unbelievable, guys who'd played a lot of hard sports said they'd never felt anything like it, the sudden drop and rocket rush of the hit, the reserves of adrenaline you could make available to yourself, pumping it up and putting it out until you were lost floating in it, not afraid, almost open to clear orgasmic death-by-drowning in it, actually relaxed. . . . Maybe you couldn't love the war and hate it inside the same instant, but sometimes those feelings alternated so rapidly that they spun together in a strobic wheel rolling all the way up until you were literally High On War, like it said on all the helmet covers. Coming off a jag like that could really make a mess out of you.[19]

These sentences rush by breathlessly, moved forward by run-on sentences, strung-out phrases, by allusions to sports and drugs and strobe lights and, especially, sex.

But any event, even one that is fairly routine, can lend itself to reflective language. Consider this description of the simple act of a police car pulling over on a highway.

> Now, in a screech of brakes, another car came onto the scene. It went by us, then spun around with squealing tires and pulled up on the far shoulder. It was a two-tone, high-speed, dome-lighted Ford, and in it was the sheriff of Laurens County. He got out and walked toward us, all

108

Technicolor in his uniform, legs striped like a pine-barrens tree frog's, plastic plate on his chest, name of Wade.[20]

These four sentences seem to move in much the same rhythm as the action they are describing. Let's look closely at them.

Sentence 1:

"Now, *in a screech of brakes,* another car came onto the scene." The sentence barely begins when it suddenly pulls itself up short, like the car, with the prepositional phrase "in a screech of brakes."

Sentence 2:

"It went by us, *then spun around with squealing tires* and pulled up on the far shoulder." This sentence pivots around its center, just as the car spins on the asphalt, then pulls up to a quiet ending, just as the car itself comes to a stop.

Sentence 3:

"It was a two-tone, high-speed, dome-lighted Ford, and in it was the sheriff of Laurens County." This sentence sashays with self-importance: a flashy self-importance in the snappy way the car is described with three quick, hyphenated adjectives; and a no-nonsense self-importance in the way its occupant is identified in the very last words. While the first two sentences were interrupted for effect, this sentence joins two independent but equally forceful clauses. It begins quietly ("It was"), crescendos to a symbol of power (the police car), begins quietly all over again ("in it was"), and crescendos to another symbol of power (the sheriff himself). This is the only sentence in the paragraph to contain all description and no action, and it serves as the anchor—the base of power—for the entire paragraph. It is the sentence around which the paragraph itself pivots.

Sentence 4:

"He got out and walked toward us, all Technicolor in his uniform, legs striped like a pine-barrens tree frog's, plastic plate on his chest, name of Wade." This sentence moves like the event being described: all the action takes place right away in the independent clause (he got out and

109

walked) and those waiting for him have a chance to size him up—just as we do as we read the subsequent description. "Name of Wade," saved for the last, not only reflects the way a trooper might talk ("Name's Wade") and offers some nice assonance (repetition of vowel sounds), but also finally introduces us to him, nailing down the paragraph with this last hard, sharp sound.

This kind of reflective language comes only with practice. There is no shortcut. While some writers may claim to do it by "instinct," those instincts need to be trained methodically, the way a dog is trained to follow a scent. Once you have the "nose" for it, then you will know in which direction to head.

Balance Long and Short

Short sentences and paragraphs tend to grab the reader more, especially when they follow long ones. On the thirtieth birthday of Disneyland, one writer chronicled the ups and downs of the amusement park with this lead:

> Thirty years ago today, on the broad oval of Southern California farm land that his bulldozers had cleared from the orange groves, Walter Elias Disney stepped up to a microphone to inaugurate an amusement park quite unlike anything anybody had ever seen before. Children would fly in this place, and cruise jungle rivers, and touch beaming cartoon creatures who had walked off the movie screens; winged galleons would sail them over London at midnight, thundering rockets would carry them to the moon, and whole freeways would fill with honking traffic, scaled precisely to their size. The streets would shine like polished nickels. Everyone in uniform would smile. "To all who come to this happy place," Disney said, gazing around him at the 30,000 people who had stormed Orange County to open his celebrated new park, "welcome."
> They had a terrible time.[21]

110

The writer begins with two long, graceful sentences that outline one man's dream. She follows them with two short sentences about the pragmatic aspects of that dream—streets would shine; employees would smile. This helps emphasize the dreamlike quality of the first two sentences. The quote at the end of the long paragraph is interrupted as Disney views his audience. While the bulk of the quote comes first, the important word—"welcome"—is saved for last.

By isolating that one word, the writer helps throw the bleak brief message of the second paragraph—"They had a terrible time"—into stark relief. These abrupt five words bring the lengthy fantasy to a harsh end.

Avoid Writing in the First Person

Some writers and editors will disagree with this. But the problem with writing in the first person is that it tends to degenerate into too many "I's"—both in the number that actually appear on the page, and in the general sense of intrusiveness upon the reader. It is difficult to write in the first person without seeming to suffer from ego inflation. It is easy to slide into "I feel" this way and "I feel" that way without the necessary supporting information to convince the reader why he or she should feel the same. It is easy to become lazy in the first person. Some great writers do write only in the first person. When you are a great writer, you can too. But when you are beginning, don't.

Some people will disregard this advice. If you must, then at least see how few "I's" you can put in your copy. When you are done with a draft, circle your "I's," then rewrite to get rid of half of them.

Eschew Bloated or Inappropriate Words

These muffle your voice and muddy your copy. There are several kinds of linguistic traps to avoid.

111

Mucky Phrases That Hide More Than They Reveal

Wars are especially fertile ground for generating an array of creative doublespeak intended to camouflage rather than reveal. Phrases like, "enhanced interrogation methods" and "collateral damage" derive from simple words and plain language: torture (in the former case), and killing of civilians (in the latter). When politicians and their spin machines commit the linguistic crime of saying such inanities, journalists should not make it worse by using them.

Handy Guide to Jargon

Try this on for size. Create a three-digit number. Using the table below, locate each number in the appropriate column in sequential order. Then read across the columns. You can create impressive and intimidating phrases such as "integrated digital concept" and "responsive monitored contingency." [22]

Column 1	Column 2	Column 3
0. integrated	0. management	0. options
1. total	1. organizational	1. flexibility
2. systematized	2. monitored	2. capability
3. parallel	3. reciprocal	3. mobility
4. functional	4. digital	4. programming
5. responsive	5. logistical	5. concept
6. optional	6. transitional	6. time-phase
7. synchronized	7. incremental	7. projection
8. compatible	8. third-generation	8. hardware
9. balanced	9. policy	9. contingency

This exercise nicely demonstrates George Orwell's contention that modern writing at its worst

> consists in gumming together long strips of words which have already been set in order by someone else, and making the results presentable by sheer humbug. The attraction of this way of writing is that it is easy. . . . If you use ready-made phrases, you not only don't have to hunt about for words, you also don't have to bother with the rhythms of your sentences, since these phrases are generally so arranged as to be more or less euphonious.[23]

Redundancies

Out of habit, people tend to be unnecessarily repetitive when speaking. However, it is crucial to be concise when writing. Watch out for phrases like these:

Avoid	Correct Usage
owned his own home	owned his home
during the winter months	during the winter
8 PM tonight	8 PM *or* 8 tonight
burned in the flames	burned
at the present time	now
consensus of opinion	consensus
disclosed for the first time	disclosed
due to the fact that	because
filled to capacity	filled
future plans	plans
gave their approval	approved
rough estimate	estimate
screamed loudly	screamed
smothered to death	smothered
revert back	revert
won a victory	won
suffocated to death	suffocated

Commonly Misused Words and Malapropisms

Lots of English words sound similar but have meanings that differ slightly or dramatically. These include words such as affect/effect; allude/elude; averse/adverse; equable/equitable.

A host of other English words sound different from one another, but seem so similar in meaning that one is inadvertently used in the other's place. These include: compose/comprise; imply/infer; less/fewer; oral/verbal.

When a word seems slippery, double-check its meaning in the dictionary.

The humorous misuse of a word is called a malapropism. You commit a malapropism when you use a word that sounds similar to another word, but is an inappropriate substitution, as in "The ships buttoned down their hatches" (instead of "battened them down"), or "it works for all intensive purposes" (instead of "for all intents and purposes").

Malapropisms are most delicious when committed by someone else. While they are often funny to read and hear, don't use them through neglect. Writing coach and author Paula LaRocque recalled a character from her childhood who said he never married because he didn't want "a grindstone around his neck," who believed that "too many cooks boil the broth," and who said that plenty of immigrants came to America because they heard that everything was "paid in gold" and as a result found themselves in a "melting pot of duck soup."[24]

Linguist Jacques Barzun recalls a Houston Oilers coach known for such malapropisms as:

- "This is the crutch of the problem." [crux]
- "We're changing our floormat." [format]
- "He has a chronicle knee injury." [chronic]

A few other classics from Barzun include:

- "Both operations were performed by the illusory Dr. B. in California." [elusive]
- "I fell for him at once—his looks, his manners: he was the perfect antithesis of a gentleman." [epitome, no doubt]
- "The suggestion was greeted with overweening disapproval." [overwhelming][25]

Turn to your dictionary not only when in doubt. Use it to double-check those words for which you are sure you know the meaning—or do you?

EXERCISES

1. Point of View
   Find a feature article that you feel contains a definite point of view even though it is not written in the first person. Analyze the writer's point of view using the following questions:

a. What is the writer's point of view toward the subject?

b. How is the writer's point of view conveyed?

c. Are there any "hidden" messages behind the quotes used in the story? What are they?

d. Does the writer use colloquialisms? If so, where? Do they help or hurt the story?

e. Pick out one of the descriptions in the story. Is the writer conveying any hidden messages through what is included or omitted? What are those messages?

f. Does the writer's voice at any point become too intrusive? Where? What is he/she doing that bothers you?

g. What techniques does he/she use that you would imitate?

2. Bad Writing

a. Rewrite this bad writing in as few words as possible.

The time taken to fall asleep in healthy males and females of all ages averages about twenty minutes. Waking should occur spontaneously. The need for an artificial awakening device indicates that there has been insufficient sleep, and the individual will suffer for it with reduced alertness during the waking period that follows.[26]

b. Rewrite this good writing from the Old Testament (Ecclesiastes) into bad modern English.

I returned, and saw under the sun, that the race is not to the swift, nor the battle to the strong, neither yet bread to the wise, nor yet riches to men of understanding, nor yet favour to men of skill; but time and chance happeneth to them all.[27]

3. Nuts and Bolts: Grammar and Spelling

How tight are your sentences? How good is your grammar?

a. Cut unnecessary words from these expressions:

- throughout the entire night
- currently serving a 20-year sentence
- gave birth to a little baby girl
- set an all-time school record

- owns a private beach
- an autopsy to determine the cause of death
- at the corner of Mercer and Bleecker streets
- the fact that she had been warned
- will revert back in 100 years
- four complimentary passes
- the other alternative
- the incumbent senator
- was totally destroyed
- an annual meeting every year
- elected by an overwhelming landslide vote

b. Many (or perhaps all) of these words contain spelling errors. Correct as necessary.[28]

seperation	excercise	flourescent
accomodate	pasttime	drunkeness
occasion	parrallel	transend
publicly	neccessary	judgment
embarass	desperate	maintainance
subpoena	committment	homicide
wierd	aquit	licence
achieve	alot (many)	mispell
alright	predominately	newstand
ecstacy	withheld	bookeeper
suprise	occurred	Carribean
reknowned	alchoholic	similiar
ommission	recommend	tyrrany
agression		

c. Correct the errors in the following sentences. Then (and only then) see how well you did by checking them against the Associated Press Managing Editor (APME) Association's guide to the most common errors in newspaper writing (see appendix).

1. Winning the lottery had a significant affect on her life.

2. I am adverse to anything that seems unethical.

3. The city is composed of the very rich and the very poor.
4. He is different than his father.
5. There were cushions on either side of the couch.
6. The body laid in state for two days.
7. She made a verbal promise.
8. Over 10,000 fans cheered the Rangers.
9. It's the principal of the thing.
10. Although they urged him to speak, he was reluctant.
11. The teacher refuted the child's claims.
12. She never knew who's fault it was.
13. Now, he had less reasons to be optimistic.
14. Hopefully, the hottest days are past.
15. She alluded the robber.

NOTES

[1] Molly Ivins, *The New York Times,* September 30, 1976.
[2] Guy Trebay, *Village Voice,* October 8, 1983.
[3] Charlotte Curtis, *The New York Times*, February 25, 1986.
[4] Joan Didion, *The New York Times Book Review,* December 5, 1976.
[5] From *Writers at Work:* The Paris Review *Interviews,* George Plimpton, Ed., Second Series (New York: Viking Press, 1963).
[6] From *Writers at Work:* The Paris Review *Interviews,* George Plimpton, Ed., Third Series (New York: Viking Press, 1967).
[7] Due to the age of the first edition, the authors do not have the publication information for this article. However, because of the usefulness and pertinent nature of this particular example, the analysis was retained for the second edition.
[8] Joan Didion, Op. cit.
[9] William Geist, *The New York Times,* April 25, 1984.
[10] Greta Tilley, *Greensboro News & Record* (NC), May 2, 1984.
[11] Guy Trebay, *Village Voice,* October 2, 1984.
[12] William Geist, *The New York Times,* November 28, 1984.
[13] Wesley Stout, James E. Knowles, and Angelo DeBernardo, *Fort Lauderdale News and Sun-Sentinel* (FL).
[14] All quotes from John McPhee appear in "Travels in Georgia," in *The John McPhee Reader* (New York: Farrar, Straus and Giroux, 1982), pp. 267–309.
[15] Michael T. Kaufman, *The New York Times,* May 20, 1986.
[16] John Hersey, *Hiroshima* (New York: Vintage, 1989).

[17] Bob Dart, *Atlanta Journal-Constitution*, August 22, 1982.

[18] Brian Ojanpa, *Free Press* (MN), June 20, 1987.

[19] Michael Herr, *Dispatches* (New York: Alfred A. Knopf, 2009), pp. 58–59.

[20] John McPhee, Op. cit.

[21] Cynthia Gorney, *The Washington Post*, July 17, 1985.

[22] Paul St. Pierre, *Williams Lake Tribune* (Canada), April 9, 1971.

[23] George Orwell, *In Front of Your Nose, 1945–1950: Collected Essays, Journalism and Letters*, Sonia Orwell and Ian Angus, Eds. (New Hampshire: Godine, 2000), p. 134.

[24] From Paula LaRocque, writing coach, author, communications consultant, former assistant managing editor, writing coach, and columnist, *Dallas Morning News*.

[25] Jacques Barzun, *Simple and Direct* (New York: Harper Perennial, 4th edition, 2001).

[26] Desmond Morris, *The Naked Ape* (New York: McGraw-Hill, 1967), pp. 111–112.

[27] For George Orwell's try at this, Op. cit.

[28] List developed by Sonia Jaffe Robbins, managing editor of *Publishers Weekly,* writer, and teacher.

The Weave

Chapter

7

The standard news story uses the inverted pyramid form: most important information on top, least important on the bottom. The feature story, however, has no intrinsic shape. It must be pieced together like a puzzle. It must be plotted like a game of chess. This refusal to be married faithfully to one form makes the shape of the feature difficult to control: it is why some respected news reporters never become great, or even good, feature writers. For in addition to the "craft" of reporting, which can to a large extent be learned, it takes an added instinct for rooting out the right words with all the compulsive single-mindedness of a bee after honey. It also takes a delight in the language, a delight so strong that it compensates for the torment of wrestling with words.

However, the feature does have many *component parts* that remain consistent, even though the final shape of each feature may be different. Previous chapters have addressed some of them: the *lead* (chapter 1), *transitions* (chapter 2), *verbs* (chapter 3), *description* (chapter 4), and *quotes* (chapter 5). This chapter is about additional basic tools you can use to help weave these parts together.

1. The *Nut*
2. The *Anecdote*
3. The *Synopsis*
4. Boring But Important *(BBI)* Information
5. The *End*

These components, blended together, give body and texture to the feature. However, remember that it is the *way* they

119

are incorporated into the story that makes them enhance or hinder the story. They should, at best, propel the story forward; at worst, they should not obstruct the story for too long.

Writing, in general, is divided into two basic types: narration and exposition.

"Narration" is the term used to describe events presented in chronological order. It is a time sequence that gives forward motion to a story. Narration implies some movement through time. Some feature components—such as the quote and the anecdote—can be used as narrative devices.

"Exposition" is the term used to describe the halt of a story to give it depth and breadth. *Description,* the *nut,* the *synopsis,* and *boring but important information* such as statistics can all be used as expository devices. The challenge is to weave the narration and exposition in such a way that the story holds solidly together. If it is constructed strong and well, it will grow old gracefully.

The essential elements of the weave described below remain the same whether you are writing for the printed page or online. However, when writing for the Web, maintain quality but modify presentation. Your weave should be tighter and shorter (see chapter 10).

The Nut

The nut is a sentence or a paragraph ("nut graf") that hooks the reader in and tells the reader "in a nutshell" *what the story is about.* It is often different from the lead. The lead gets the reader into the story, but does not always convey the full context of the story unless the writer has resorted to a standard news lead (see chapter 1).

Generally, however, the feature lead is not expected to say what the story is about. Its primary function is to lure the reader *into* the story. Because of this, at some point early in the story, the writer must figuratively stand back, take the reader by the hand, and say: "Now, dear reader, I am going to tell you the gist of this story." This is the nut, the nugget, the distillation, the linguistic gem.

In shorter features (say, 300–500 words), and for features on the Web, the nut is more likely to appear soon after the first paragraph. In longer magazine-length features, it may appear deeper in the story. By this time, the reader is usually engaged enough in the story to keep on reading.

The nut should be clear, simple, to the point. While you may not want to reveal *all* (you may, for instance, want to hold in reserve a surprise twist for near the end), you must reveal enough to be fair to the story.

The nut graf is the only place in the story where you have an *obligation* to intrude deliberately on the story and inform the reader of what is to come. No matter how complex your subject, it need be only a few words long.

For example, after a lively descriptive lead about the antics of ninth graders in a Florida school, the writer gets to the heart of the matter in his nut graf, with eight simple words standing alone:

Ninth grade is where it all falls apart.

He is signaling the reader about what's next: this story is an in-depth look at the educational and personal challenges unique to those in their early teens. This is a tricky moment in his feature. Most people do not want to read about big social problems, and will stop right here. But he is a writer who knows his craft. In the sentence following the nut, he deliberately recruits vivid imagery and powerful verbs, creating an energy that helps keep the reader going:

> [Ninth grade is] a wall, a window, a mirror. It's where thousands of 14- and 15-year-olds, blindly hurtling toward adulthood, run smack into something they can't knock down and can't climb over. They fail. They turn 16. They quit.[1]

Through strength of language and detail, he eases readers into the story, immersing them painlessly into some painful issues.

There are no hard and fast rules for where you should plant the nut in your story. This feature on a new political appointment takes a very different, but also effective, approach. The first sentence is the lead. The second sentence contains the nut, but it is wrapped inside information selected by the writer to keep the story moving:

> After only a few hours on the job yesterday, the new warden of the Bronx Men's House of Detention had been blown a kiss by one inmate and been called "beautiful" by another. [*lead*]
>
> But Gloria Viola Lee, who on Monday became the first woman in the city's history to head a men's prison [*nut*], made it clear very quickly that such endearments did not matter one way or another as far as running her prison was concerned.[2]

The real hook, or nut, here—that this story is about the first woman to head a men's prison in New York City—is smoothly woven inside a sentence that keeps us focused on the subject's personality. It keeps a "breakthrough" story on the personal level, making it more engaging. The rest of the feature is about Ms. Lee's professional background, her attitude toward her new job, and other inmates' reactions.

When writing your nut graf, do not present too many facts too soon. You can save some basic information—especially statistics and background—for later. If you reveal all of your hand at the start, it may slow down entry into the story and undermine any motivation to read to the end. However, if you withhold too much for too long, you will also lose the reader, who will quickly begin to wonder what the story is about.

There is no exact formula for how much to put in the nut graf: use common sense and follow your instincts, which will improve with practice.

The Anecdote

The anecdote is a re-creation of an event, an incident, or an interaction that may include description, quotes, or background. It usually (but not always) involves a dynamic between two or more people that can be used to illustrate a point in the story—a mood, a predicament, a dilemma, a person's beliefs or experiences. It can range from a sentence to several paragraphs.

The great attraction of anecdotes is that by re-creating an event they move the story forward through time; they tell "mini-stories" within the larger story, which helps keep it moving along.

Many beginning writers tend to overlook anecdotes when they sit down to write, either because they haven't gathered enough detail to develop a good anecdote, or because they don't yet have the patience or skills to shape the anecdote in a way that will fit smoothly into the story. Anecdotes are hard to develop and present well, but they are worth the effort.

In the following example, the psychic scars inflicted by two drug addicts are captured in one-line anecdotes.

One addict is the mother of a 1-year-old child. While a sister is trying to get custody, the child, increasingly passive and withdrawn, continues to live with her mother. The writer uses an anecdote to convey the impact of this addiction on the child:

> When her mother drifted off into a narcotic haze, Jennifer would crawl into her lap and sit there for hours, as if to protect her.

The other addict, a young man, is first described this way by the writer:

He had always considered himself something of a physical specimen. Lean and blond, just over six feet tall, he pumped iron and practiced a strict regimen of karate throughout adolescence. That was the old Robert Black.

Then, the writer gives an anecdote:

The new Robert Black was so debilitated by heroin that when he wrestled with his mother over a syringe she found under a sofa in her apartment, he lost.[3]

Anecdotes can also be powerful metaphors. In the story below about the decay of the Acropolis in Greece from pollution, the writer uses a seven-sentence anecdote about one elderly tourist from Worcester, Massachusetts, to convey the mortality of men and monuments. The writer describes the ailing man's last visit to the Parthenon:

He told the taxi driver to wait for him. As he started up the path, he reflected that the Acropolis might be mortal after all. When the doctors told him last August that he had cancer and probably would not live past January, he had wrestled with his faith and come to terms with his own mortality. But, having survived his deadline, he decided to take advantage of the extra days to photograph the Parthenon one more time. He had earned his living as a photographer and had photographed it on many previous visits in all kinds of light and weather.

But as he struggled up the incline toward the Acropolis, he realized that he did not have the strength to complete the climb. He turned back toward the taxi, and when he finally got his breath, he remarked to the driver, "It's probably better to remember it as it was."[4]

This anecdote raises some questions: How did the writer happen to be there when this man got out of his taxi? How did he know what he was thinking as he walked up to the Parthenon? Perhaps he was a friend, relative, or acquaintance. Perhaps they shared the taxi, or just happened to arrive at the same time. Perhaps this man confided his history and his fears to the writer before the visit, or after. Or perhaps the writer had to pry them out of him through cautious questioning.

Anecdotes are elusive: you must find them; they won't rush to you. In the above anecdote, for example, the writer in

Greece recognized the possibilities intrinsic in the situation; he saw the juncture between two seemingly disparate subjects—the slow death of a human being and a building—and used it.

Good anecdotes take good timing, good reporting, good instincts, and patience. They do not spring out at you; instead, you usually have to eke them out from the bits and pieces of your story. And you have to know them when you see them. In the Parthenon story, the writer's radar was scanning for signals, for symbols of the moment—and found one.

The Synopsis

In a complex story, the synopsis—condensation of lengthy information—becomes essential.

A background in standard news reporting often helps here. After researching a story, the writer should be awash in information. It usually comes in dribs and drabs, unclear, incomplete, often redundant, sometimes superfluous, exaggerated, or misleading. It is the writer's job to sift through and winnow it, and then compress it into some palatable shape (the briefer the better) that the reader can swallow painlessly. The longer the feature, the more often a writer will have to stop the story for a synopsis.

Synopses are especially useful tools in a controversy, in public events (ranging from courtroom trials to community meetings and annual celebrations), and in personal events related during a lengthy interview.

Controversy

Opposing views should be presented quickly, without allowing grandstanding by either side.

Here, for instance, is a synopsis of different views on the way to reduce the incidence of violent juvenile crime:

> There is a disagreement about how to best deal with the problem. Police talk of harsher penalties with more incar-

125

ceration while child welfare advocates look for ways to reduce or even end imprisonment.[5]

The writer then goes on to discuss each view in detail.

Here is a synopsis of a battle in the 1980s in Robeson County, North Carolina, over construction of two toxic water-treatment plants, one of them for radioactive waste:

> The residents contend that their area was selected for the plants because it has a median family income about half the national average and has historically wielded little political power, and because more than half of the people are black or American Indian.
>
> Spokesmen for GSX and US Ecology say the area was selected because it provided the best facilities for their plants. They both insist the plants pose no health threats to the area and categorically deny that the sites were political choices.[6]

Public Events

City council sessions, trials, award presentations, parent-teacher meetings, annual celebrations—all tend to be messy from the writer's point of view. There's too much detail, too much trivia, and too much repetition. A common problem in covering them is that the resulting story is not tight enough. Because the writer faces so much redundancy, the decisions about what to put in and what to exclude become more difficult. In covering public events, the writer must be merciless in chopping away all nonessential information, and must be sharp enough to find and highlight the most revealing and pertinent facts—and nothing else.

When Atlanta first committed millions of dollars to develop the Underground Atlanta "marketplace" in the center of the city, it was promised that at least 25 percent of the 150 businesses there would be minority-owned. Here is a summation of a meeting between the developer—the Rouse Company—and minority business people in city hall:

> To start fulfilling its promise, Rouse took part in a presentation at City Hall last week. Roughly 150 people, from gelato scoopers to body shop owners, crowded the council chambers to hear company and city officials tell what it takes to get a piece of the action.
>
> Mainly, money.
>
> More than a few faces dropped when the Rouse man started talking about investments of $50,000 to $1 million.
>
> Herman Pittman, who sells chicken wings out of a catering wagon called Uncle Herman's Cabin, says he has less than $10,000 in the bank. "Underground is fixed against the grassroots minorities," he said. "These people want such a foolproof package, they're going to end up with only the handpicked elite blacks who are tapped into the system."[7]

This is an effective synopsis for several reasons: First, although 150 business people were at the meeting, the writer conveys the *type* of small businesses represented by mentioning only *three* of them: gelato scoopers, body shop owners, and a chicken wing vendor. That's enough.

Second, he highlights *one* high-impact moment: the instant when the developer gave the bottom-line numbers needed to open a business. He sums up the general reaction: "more than a few faces dropped." That, again, is enough when backed up by a quote from one of those dropped faces.

And third, in the final paragraph, he uses *one* quote (although he undoubtedly gleaned many, many more from the disappointed and outraged audience). The quote, it is safe to bet, is a pithy reflection of the way many people felt.

And last, but most important, the synopsis is well written. The two-word paragraph—"Mainly, money"—stands out from the longer paragraphs and sentences. Each sentence is important to the piece; there is no self-indulgence here.

Trial Reporting

Trial reporting calls on special skills in summarizing hours or even months of testimony. While Brooke Astor, the wealthy socialite and philanthropist, suffered from Alzheimer's disease, her son was accused of stealing from her $185 million estate by doctoring her wills. Here is a synopsis of the courtroom proceedings:

> Fifteen weeks, 65 witnesses, 11,000 pages of testimony—
> and prosecutors in the Brooke Astor fraud trial still aren't
> done presenting their case.
>
> Determined to prove that Astor's son, Anthony Marshall, and his pal Francis Morrissey plundered the senile socialite's $185 million fortune, they have put on the stand witness, after witness, after witness, after witness, after witness.
>
> Overkill?
>
> Legal eagles say the glazed eyes and yawns of some of the jurors should be setting off alarms for prosecutors.
>
> "There's no way the jury is going to remember what the fifth witness, for example, said," said defense lawyer Joseph Tacopina, who is not involved in the Astor case.
>
> "Even if the witness is Henry Kissinger."
>
> The longer the trial goes on, the more it tries the jury's patience, he said.
>
> "When you take four months to present your case, you also run the risk of [angering] the jury," Tacopina said.[8]

In this synopsis, the writers chose two tools that help keep the story moving. First, they keep the sentences, descriptions, quotes, and paragraphs short. The single word question, "Overkill?" packs a particular punch.

Second, they take advantage of several tools described in this book to reveal in an easy-to-read way the underlying tedium of a highly publicized trial: a tight factual lead that uses just two statistics to show scope (number of witnesses, pages of testimony); repetition to evoke interminable hours in the courtroom ("witness, after witness, after witness, after witness, after witness"); brevity in adjectives (eyes are "glazed"), verbs (money is "plundered"), and colloquialisms (lawyers are "legal eagles"); and a sprinkling of quotes from experts who reinforce the message the reporters wish to send.

And despite the trial's tedium, the accused were found guilty.

Recurring Events

Feature writers are often asked to cover parades, festivals, fund-raisers, and other events that present the special challenge of how to find something new and fresh to say about activities that are written up every year. The power of language goes a long way toward compensating for the boredom of the familiar.

Here is a synopsis of Frontier Day, which for more than 100 years has been an annual celebration in Cheyenne, Wyoming:

> The Cheyenne townsfolk prepare 3,000 pounds of ham and more than 100,000 pancakes each year for the 30,000 people that show up. They mix the pancake batter in a cement truck and you'll have to sit on a bale of hay. But the price is right and nobody waits more than 20 minutes. Wyoming breakfasts—a shot of whiskey and a chaw of tobacco—are optional.[9]

Just a few well-chosen details—the pounds of ham; the number of pancakes; the cement truck used to mix pancake batter; the whiskey-and-tobacco breakfast (with, note, the colloquial expression "chaw of tobacco")—suffice to arouse interest.

Or, in the following example, the students at a junior high school compete against their teachers in their annual basketball game. Here, the reasons for the game's popularity are summarized, followed by a quick synopsis of student dialogue to help illustrate the ambiance surrounding the event:

> They love the game for so many reasons, among them:
> - The opportunity to see teachers in shorts.
> - The camaraderie of the court, which allows them to drop deference and proper titles, to wit, "Take the train, Epstein," "Get a haircut, Rudy," and the obligatory, "Nice hands, Herschkowitz," uttered only when Mr. Herschkowitz has either flubbed a dribble or a basket. The students also get a lot of satisfaction out of shrieking "child abuse" when a

129

member of their team is fouled and "police brutality" if the foul is committed by Officer Trifeletti.
- The fair exchange of criticism, mostly against Mr. Silkowitz, who, in all fairness, must be said to occasionally foul other players with impunity.

"Silkowitz is a butcher," said one student.

"He's a nice guy," said a fair-minded player.

"But he's a butcher," said a third.

"Who are you talking about, Silkowitz, right?" said someone, sticking his head into the circle by the bleachers.

"He'd probably be good at football," said one of the others.

"Part of his bad reputation is because he's assistant principal," said the fair-minded one.

"I'm known for my aggressive style," said Mr. Silkowitz in response.[10]

With synopses, writers rely on their skills as linguistic surgeons to excise the excess verbiage and get on with the story.

Personal Events

Some synopses focus on a specific, often cathartic, life event that is pivotal to a person's current goals, beliefs, or problems. They are written snapshots that reverse the adage that a picture is worth a thousand words. Instead, a dozen well-chosen words are worth a thousand pictures.

Again, the writer's challenge is to select the right moments and then re-create them in a brief, vivid way. People who are talking about special moments in their lives tend to be either verbose or nearly inarticulate about what happened and why it meant so much. Their memories may be hazy. They are rarely concise. It is up to the writer to condense and focus.

Here, in only two paragraphs, Habitat for Humanity founder Millard Fuller recalls how his wife's threat to leave him changed his life:

Unfortunately, Fuller, always thinking of the next deal, was consumed by his work. Even when he was home, he wasn't really there—until, one day, Mrs. Fuller precipitated the key crisis in his life by confronting him with a sad fact: She was leaving him because he seemed more in love with money than his family.

Always a religious man and the founder of a United Church of Christ in Montgomery, Fuller was stunned. Never one to go halfway, he sold his business, gave his money away and started over, eventually bringing his family to Sumter County, Georgia, and Koinonia, an interracial Christian farming commune founded by New Testament scholar Clarence Jordan in 1942.[11]

Or a writer may pluck from a person's past *a few* details to highlight those things that best symbolize the person in the context of the story. A doctor's popularity in his community is illuminated with two taut synopses following the lead:

He is a doctor who knows his patients.

He knows about Mr. Smith's allergy to penicillin and the Atlanta Braves and about his fear of not being able to keep up with the younger men on the job.

He knows about the weak tissue around Mrs. Jones' right elbow, the weakness she has for persimmon pudding and the way she became weak-kneed when her daughter who wanted to go anywhere ran off with the man who recruited her to sell magazines.[12]

The meltdowns of professional athletes usually hit the media, even if they are less well known than, say, the golfer Tiger Woods. After the dust settles, it is up to the feature writer to give us context, perspective, and insight into the personal trauma behind the public drama. In this feature on a once-promising professional golf champion, the writer leans on a few precise details and a short quote from a former college coach to foreshadow the champion's self-destruction:

On the golf course, he was a brilliant manipulator of the ball—"He could hit it in his sleep," says [coach] Nardi-ello. But [golfer] Thomas also enjoyed playing the role of the renegade—snubbing his nose at any authority figure he could find. By the time he got to college, Thomas was a heavy pot smoker and drinker. While other players arrived at away matches with luggage and clubs, Thomas arrived with luggage and clubs and a case of Heineken.[13]

Boring But Important (BBI) Information

BBI information includes statistics, official reports, and general background. Almost every story has some of this, and the problem is always how to fold it into the feature without coming to a dead stop. Whenever possible, weave BBI information into the middle of other, more interesting, information. Usually, the lower down in the story you put the BBI information, the better off you will be. If you have a lot of this type of information, it is usually better to scatter it throughout the story, so that it doesn't appear as one big block of dead weight.

Statistics

Keep statistics to a minimum, as they are hard to digest. If the statistics are alarming or striking, then by all means use them but be brief and direct.

If you have lots of statistics, it is a good idea to build them into the infrastructure of the story. Notice how, in the following article about a bingo game in the Mashantucket Pequot Indian Reservation in Connecticut, the writer manages to personalize the statistics by blending them with the action of a "typical" day, and uses healthy verbs, most of them in the present tense, to move along the story:

> Nothing has done more for the reservation lately than bingo. The game started in July 1986 and is taking in about $10 million a year, providing about $2 million—half the tribe's income—in profit.
>
> Every day but Tuesday and Wednesday, 800 to 1,000 people arrive here, often by chartered bus from as far as

New York and Maine, and pay $25 to $150 for admission into the reservation's $4.6 million bingo hall.

There, they spend up to five hours blotting out letters and numbers on scorecards, hoping to win anywhere from $50 to $2,000 per game, and occasionally more. Much more.

Two weeks ago, Lorraine Milolinski, a housewife from Cheshire, won $22,000. "I really went bananas," she said.[14]

Nearly every sentence here is providing statistics, but it seems painless for two reasons: first, the writer focuses on what happens on an average day; and second, he wraps the numbers inside action sentences that move the reader forward and end on a high note: gamblers arrive on the bus, spend five hours in the casino, blot out letters and numbers, and sometimes win.

Official Reports

Many stories require writers to slog through official reports and then summarize them for the reader. Usually, the briefer the summary, the better.

In a feature on a barber school, the writer sums up the course catalog in one long sentence:

The catalogue describes the exhaustive curriculum of 1,000 hours, usually accomplished over six months, which includes classes in such subjects as thinning shears, pompadours, the part, use of the towel, shaving the neck, methods of rinsing, shop ventilation, personal hygiene, shop management, first aid, and the patron-barber relationship.[15]

However, it sometimes livens up a story to have a small portion of an official report quoted verbatim. While the report may be boring as a whole, you can incorporate part of it into your story in a way that is not.

For this article on Disneyland, the writer plucked out some graphic details from the park's maintenance report:

Park Defects Reports, issued daily for overnight repair work, July 4 and 7, partial list:

Cigar store Indian needs touch up.

Gate that leads to Mad Hatter does not swing back to close after opening.

Thatching coming off roof of Mad Hatter above east door. All brass "Watch Your Step" signs need polish.

Water buffalo python scene sensor not triggering—currently on override.[16]

General Background

Most stories need some background to add perspective. Background includes personal history (birthplace, parents, education, jobs) or public history (the environmental record of a corporation, the ups and downs of a school system, the track record of the last governor). Often, personal and public histories merge in a feature background.

There are three rules of thumb for inserting general background:

1. Put it in chronological order.

2. Begin it about one-third of the way into the story.

3. Keep it tight, tight, tight.

Each of these rules, however, may be bent or broken. Since each story has its own personality, it is important to let the content guide the structure, rather than the other way around.

The End

While it is all right for a traditional news story to just drift away in the end, the last paragraph of a feature story should be as compelling as the first. It is important for nonfiction to have "closure," to end as definitely as a sonnet or a play. One good technique for closure is to make the story come full circle and end with an echo of your lead. This kind of ending literally "wraps up" your story by tying the end to the beginning.

For example, here is the lead and then the end to a feature on the final destination of some of the urban poor. The story begins:

> The man who was born in Hungary was the oldest. He had lived in a single-room-occupancy hotel and died in the hospital. He was 83 years old.
>
> The next man was 82. He lived in the same kind of hotel and had a sister living upstate.
>
> The third was 51 and lived in a narrow little place on the Bowery, with a bar on the bottom floor. His sister lived in the city, and came to the funeral mass. So did one of his buddies, who fell over in a pew, drunk, and cajoled a nun into giving him some spare change.
>
> The boy was 15. He was born in Bellevue Hospital, and he lived and died there, plagued by imaginary demons that seemed terribly real to him. He hanged himself with a strong length of cloth, and the nurses arranged to have him buried. He had no known relatives.
>
> None of them knew the others. Very few people still living, apparently, had known any of them. On a clear autumn afternoon, with the sky like soft-blue cotton flannel, the four of them were buried in the same grave, one pressed wood coffin atop the other.

The writer goes on to describe the cemetery for the poor and unclaimed. After a quote from the grave digger, the story then ends with a new litany:

> "You have four today and you might have four next week. You got to be ready for them."
>
> They were ready for them. The hole had already been dug for four more when they buried the four on that blue afternoon. And sure enough, the following week there were indeed four more.
>
> The oldest was an 88-year-old Italian immigrant who had died in a nursing home in Manhattan.

The next was a 57-year-old derelict who lived in the Bowery.

The third was from the Bowery, too, and was 58 years old. The fourth was a man who had lived in a tiny room on the Upper West Side and died in St. Luke's Hospital. None of them knew the others.[17]

Repetition of sentence structure (each set includes "the oldest," "the next," "the third") and even an entire sentence ("None of them knew the others") increases the sad sense of inevitability in this story.

Because the feature story need not follow a straight chronology from beginning to end, it is also possible to have the lead and the end reflect *the same moment in time,* with the entire story then built around that moment.

Here, for instance, is the lead on the story about the blessing of the animals during the feast of St. Francis of Assisi:

Dogs barked in the nave of the Cathedral of St. John the Divine on Sunday, and no one troubled to quiet them. Poodle, dachshund, Pomeranian, Labrador, and mutt, all were invited guests at an annual celebration for the feast of St. Francis of Assisi.

The writer then spends 900 words describing the animals and a few of their owners. He ends the story just as the ceremony is about to begin:

The heavy doors opened, and the dark aisle was lit with columns of sunshine. Bits of fur blew inward. There was a hush, and a communal gasp as the elephant hove into view. Wherever you looked were humans embracing their pets, humbly expressing relationships that transcended ritual and were purely Franciscan. From the street, a lone voice carried dimly into the cathedral. "Free the elephant," howled an anti-vivisectionist named Teresa Rivezzo. "Set all animals free."[18]

136

However you choose to end, make the ending strong. Make it impossible for the editor to chop from the bottom. Make your story worth reading to the very last word.

Then stop.

EXERCISES

1. Print out a feature of 1,000–1,500 words covering one of the following general areas:

   - tragedy (the aftermath of a deadly crime; promise ruined by a scandal or drugs; the death, disability, or suffering of a young person)
   - light human interest (an unusual person or offbeat place or event)
   - a serious social issue (the economy, racism, the environment, crime)

   Now take it apart to see what makes it tick. Discuss your answers with friends or classmates.

   a. Where is the nut? How deep is it inside the story? Does it work well there?

   b. Does the author use anecdotes? If so, where are they? How do they add to the story?

   c. What does the writer synopsize (controversy, public events, a trial, recurring events, personal events)? How tightly are the synopses written? Could any of them have been cut without damaging the story?

   d. How is BBI information handled here? Where are statistics, reports, and general background placed in the story? Are they intrusive? If not, why not?

   e. Are the lead and end both appropriate? Does the end mirror the lead? Does it "wrap up" the story in an effective way?

   f. What is the author's voice here? How is it manifested?

   g. Does this story move fast or slowly? Does its pacing suit the subject matter? What role do transitions play in the pacing? What role do verbs play?

h. How many quotes are used? Does each one add something important to the story? If so, what? Could any be paraphrased?

i. Do the sentences in this story tend to be long, short, or mixed? Choose two of the paragraphs you feel are particularly well written, and identify the literary techniques that are used to make them successful.

2. Choose a second news feature that is vastly different in topic and tone from your choice in exercise 1.

   a. Analyze this feature using the same questions given above.

   b. How do the two stories differ? How are they the same? How does the different structure reflect the difference in subject matter?

   c. Which feature do you feel is better? Why?

3. Repeat the above for a feature you have written.

NOTES

[1] Ron Matus, *St. Petersburg Times* (FL), December 10, 2006.

[2] Judith Cummings, *The New York Times*, November 9, 1978.

[3] Stephen Braun, *Detroit Free Press*, February 7, 1983.

[4] Nicholas Gage, *The New York Times*, June 23, 1978.

[5] Raad Cawthon, *Atlanta Journal-Constitution*, February 17, 1987.

[6] Philip Shabecoff, *The New York Times*, April 1, 1986.

[7] Jim Auchmutey, *Atlanta Journal-Constitution*, June 28, 1987.

[8] Melissa Grace and Corky Siemaszko, *New York Daily News*, August 4, 2009.

[9] John Aloysius Farrell, *Washington Post*, July 13, 1986.

[10] Anna Quindlen, *The New York Times*, March 9, 1983.

[11] Keith Graham, *Atlanta Journal-Constitution*, March 10, 1987.

[12] Greta Tilley, *Greensboro News & Record* (NC), October 5, 1986.

[13] Amy Ellis Nutt, *Star-Ledger* (NJ), August 31, 2003.

[14] Nick Ravo, *The New York Times* Service, *International Herald Tribune*, December 7, 1987.

[15] William Geist, *The New York Times*, June 22, 1985.

[16] Cynthia Gorney, *Washington Post*, July 17, 1985.

[17] Anna Quindlen, *The New York Times*, October 24, 1983.

[18] Guy Trebay, *Village Voice*, October 15, 1985.

Doing It

The act of writing begins long before you sit down in front of your computer. Writing is, in fact, only one of six steps needed to produce a good feature article. The steps are:

1. Getting the Idea
2. Researching
3. Clearing Your Mind
4. Organizing
5. Writing
6. Editing

Getting the Idea

Some students and beginning writers get stuck at this stage. While most nonfiction writers are brimming with ideas, others freeze when asked to come up with them. Their minds go blank. They cannot think of a single interesting thing to write about, even in the middle of New York City.

To be a successful feature writer, you must be able to generate and "pitch" your own ideas. This is true even for writers employed full time by online and printed publications. Ideas for features come from many sources, but *you* are, in effect, the primary initiator of ideas; *you* must be receptive to the story possibilities intrinsic in almost any situation.

Anna Quindlen, who won a Pulitzer Prize for her *New York Times* columns, once explained:

> The question I am asked most often is where I come up with my ideas. The answer is that it depends on what is

uppermost in the news. That is, if my car is towed, I do a
column about car towing. If I have a tetanus shot, I do a
column about hospital emergency rooms. If I am dis-
gusted with the subways, I do a column on the subways.
This is why I have done so many subway columns.[1]

Quindlen also just walked around the city, storing up the
minutia of daily life, saving it for the day when it might be
used in a feature.

Notice that her definition of "the news" is "things that
happen in my life." While not all feature writers have the luxury of researching and writing about what is uppermost in
their minds at the moment, her basic instincts apply to all good
feature writers: you find stories with which people can *identify.*

Be a Perpetual Student

Feature writers are like perpetual students. Every story is
an excuse to learn something new. To succeed, you must have
the instincts of the Renaissance person: sweeping curiosity, a
desire to track down answers, an enthusiasm for the unknown.
Look for stories that are about "hot" topics, stories that arouse
curiosity, stories that are often overlooked.

Stay tuned into everything. If you are writing for local
publications, keep your ears open for the gossip, squabbles,
and changes in your neighborhood and campus. Even if you
are aiming for wider markets, the problems and concerns of
your friends and colleagues are often a reflection of broader
regional or national events as well.

If you want to write for a print magazine, remember that most work three to six months in advance, so you need to consider what will be on the reader's mind at the time of publication. If you're brainstorming story ideas in January you need to think summer, not snow.

Suck Up Information

Read as much as possible, and know what is being written about in online and offline publications ranging from *People* to the *Wall Street Journal*. Read recent nonfiction books in your areas of interest. Surf the Web, casting your net at a variety of social networking sites (such as Twitter, Facebook, or other popular sites) where you can gather ideas, information, and points of view (also check sites like YouTube, Craigslist, or a plethora of blogs). Set up alerts on Google or other popular search engines so you can receive news headlines, audio, and video in your areas of interest.

Watch news and features on public television and listen to public radio. Commercial cable and radio talk shows often shed more heat than light, but are useful for hearing opinions across the full political spectrum. The persons interviewed and subjects discussed can trigger ideas for other stories; they are also a reflection of what is considered (at least by producers and editors) to be topical.

Keep a record of ideas before they slip away. When you find an online article or link of interest, bookmark it in an "ideas" folder on your computer. Tear out printed articles and put them in a hard copy file on your shelf.

Story ideas are found everywhere. Look for them on eBay and other online marketplaces, special interest magazines, bulletin boards, community newspapers, meeting minutes, activist group newsletters, local government Web sites, college newspapers, police auctions, or U.S. Census Bureau reports.

Above all, keep your eyes and ears open. Be curious. Notice conversations while waiting in lines and riding elevators. Value the incidents that happen to you, your friends, your neighbors. If you are worried about the job market or a friend in the military or how to be more "green," so are your potential readers. You never know what might spark the next story idea.

Researching

The amount of research you can do for your feature depends on your deadline and the type of publication to which you plan to pitch the idea. If you're on assignment and writing for a Web site or daily newspaper, you may have only a few hours to read the "clips" (previous stories on the topic), to use search engines for additional information, and to make a few phone calls.

If you are preparing a query letter, or your assignment is not due for weeks, then you have time to do more extensive research and reporting. Research takes time and patience, but is essential to the final quality and credibility of your story. Keep in mind that research takes several forms:

- **Online:** Begin with search engines and look for articles, studies, books, conferences, experts, background material, and other information. Search widely through a variety of sources. The exercises at the end of this chapter will help familiarize you with some of the most reliable sources.

- **The library:** A professional librarian can help you design a search strategy to focus your research and find additional sources you may not know about.

- **The experts:** Find the organizations and people who are specialists in this topic. Read what they have available. Then call for an interview. They can give you inside information and other contacts.
- **The people impacted:** Through the above sources, and your own personal contacts, find people to interview who are personally involved in or impacted by your story. Interview them. These are the people who are most likely to give your story the personal touch and texture it needs.

Why spend time on research before you begin to write? Because your feature story is not an essay. It is about something bigger than just you.

Research produces for your story an angle, a focus, and a deeper understanding. It helps you avoid embarrassing mistakes and false assumptions. It gives you enough facts to write an informed, compelling, fair, and thoughtful story.

It gives you more to give your readers, and that is what will lead to your success.

Clearing Your Mind

The third step of the writing process is usually called "avoidance," "writer's block," or "procrastination."

You have done the research and reporting, you're ready to begin—but you find yourself thinking of reasons why you cannot. During this stage, writers appear to do anything not to write: they jog, shop, surf the Web, organize their music play list, rearrange the furniture, sharpen pencils, text friends, clean out the refrigerator, sleep.

Every writer feels some degree of guilt about this stage, which may last half a day, or up to a month. If it lasts longer than a week or so, then it is probably no longer a "stage" in the writing process, but is more likely a case of true procrastination.

But all writers need some time to clear their desks and their minds. While the body is otherwise occupied, the mind is preparing to write.

It is almost as if, before you tackle the story, you have to prepare for the fight. You gird yourself mentally for what is to come.

Organizing

Once you sit down to write, you need to sift through and evaluate all your material. You are trying to establish an angle for your story, and to consider the key points that you want to make. This involves a careful rereading of all your notes, which by now should be waiting for you in readable form: sloppy handwritten notes and recorded interviews should be typed up and clearly marked.

Plan to spend some time just going through all this information. Read it carefully. Highlight different themes in your notes either on a computer or on paper with different colored pens.

For longer features, type an outline of your story, and leave lots of white space to add marginal notes reminding you to add this quote here, that anecdote there.

Print a copy of the outline and tape it to your wall so you can see it. Modify it as needed.

Each writer has her or his own way of organizing information in a way that is helpful to the process of writing. You should try out different ways until you find the one that is most comfortable for you.

The point is to have some sense of the *shape* of the story before you begin writing—or very soon thereafter. The shape may change, but begin with a plan just the same.

Writing

To maximize your productivity, make sure you have at least two hours of quiet and privacy. More is better, but most writers find they can't concentrate for more than three to four hours at a stretch.

Cut Off Distractions

The phone, visitors, and e-mail will destroy your ability to work. Turn off your cell phone. Close your Web browser, e-mail, and all access to text/instant messaging.

Inform your friends, relatives, acquaintances, and associates that you will make yourself available to them before and after your working hours. Post a note on your door, asking visitors not to knock or buzz; leave paper and a pencil so they can leave you a note.

Some people find it too distracting to work in their own home. If you do, then find another space in which to write: a library, a small office, or the home of a friend who is away during your writing hours. Some people find they can concentrate in coffee shops surrounded by other kindred spirits absorbed by their laptops or personal digital devices.

Write on a Schedule

Allocate specific hours on specific days of the week for writing. Many writers like to plan to produce a certain number of pages during each writing session. If you set these kinds of goals, be sure they are reasonable and achievable. Every writer has his or her own speed, and some people write much faster than others.

If you find your goals overly ambitious, adjust them. Otherwise, you will end each writing day feeling you have failed, rather than feeling, as you should, that you have succeeded in that day's work. Keep in mind that even if you do decide to discard the results the next day, drafts that never make it past your circular file are still important stages to the final product.

Norman Mailer used to write four days a week: Mondays, Tuesdays, Thursdays, and Fridays. Each day, he would work from 10:00 AM to 12:30 PM, then have lunch, then begin writing again at 2:30 or 3:00 PM for another two hours. He tried to average seven typewritten pages a day, twenty-eight pages a week. Ernest Hemingway, who used to write standing up, would mark on a chart the exact number of words he wrote each day. If he wanted to take the next day off to go fishing, he would write a little longer until he was satisfied with his word count.[2]

The important thing is to write on a schedule. It should be part of your routine.

Then, begin at the beginning.

Don't Get Stuck on Your Lead

Try out some possible leads. If they don't work, save them, since you will probably be able to use some of them later in the body of the story.

If you have trouble getting started, some writers suggest you "speed write" your way to a lead—just start typing, as quickly as possible, whatever you think the best lead might be. Don't aim for a perfect lead the first time around. You will refine, polish, and probably even change it as you move through your story. If writing a good lead seems to be intimidating, some suggest you begin writing in what you think is the middle of your story, and then work your way backward to the lead.

Remember to write with a dictionary and a thesaurus nearby. Learn and use at least one new good word in your story.

Editing

If you're a supremely talented artist and you hit a very lucky day, then maybe you can write a poem or story or chapter or a novel that needs no revision. If you're a regular writer with your appointed portion of esthetic luck, you'll need to come at the piece again and again. I like to think of revision as a form of self-forgiveness: you can allow yourself mistakes and shortcomings in your writing because you know you're coming back later to improve it. Revision is the way you cope with the bad luck that made your writing less than brilliant this morning.[3]

A story is not finished once it is written. This does not mean you should write a story carelessly, as if it were a first draft. You should turn in a polished, professional piece if you expect to be treated as a serious professional writer.

Six Steps to Productive Editing

1. Write the story the editor expects.

To minimize the amount of editing and rewriting, it is best if you and the editor make absolutely sure you agree on the theme, tone, voice, and general substance of the article *before* you first write the story. If the theme, tone, voice, or substance changes as you gather information, tell the editor. Make an appointment if necessary, and discuss the changes in-depth *before* you begin writing. Editors hate surprises. If they are expecting a story on types of marshmallows, don't turn in a story on ways of roasting them. Give them marshmallows, unless you have arranged ahead of time to focus on this new theme.

2. Give yourself some distance.

To prepare for editing and rewriting, the first thing you should do after you finish the story is *nothing*. This means letting the story lie at least overnight, preferably a few days. Stay away from it. When you return to it, you will have fresh perspective.

3. Do your own first edits.

To the best of your ability do the first edit yourself. The most common writing problems that need to be tackled in an edit and rewrite have been discussed in this book: weak quotes, overwriting, clichés and other tired language, shaky organization, inadequate transitions, lack of color, vacillation in the writer's voice. If you are unsure if something "works,"

147

go back to earlier chapters and check your writing against the basic principles outlined there. If you are still uncertain, continue revising that part of your story until you are satisfied with it.

Before the story gets to a professional editor, many writers ask a relative, a friend, or a writer's group to read the story and evaluate it. Sometimes this can be helpful, even invaluable, if the person asked is good at editing. This kind of intervention has saved many a beginning writer from having a story rejected by an editor who didn't have the time or talent to fix it.

But calling on a friend to edit also has its pitfalls: the friend may say it's great because he or she doesn't want to hurt your feelings, or doesn't know enough about writing to identify what might be improved. If the friend can't write, he or she may be impressed by anyone who can write anything at all. So choose your "personal" editors with the same care you choose your "professional" editors.

If your mother, spouse, or sibling says it's great, and your professional editor says it has lots of problems, be inclined to believe the second opinion.

4. Trust your editor.

The talents of a professional editor are different from those of a writer: good editors are not only whizzes at grammar and the basics of language, but they are also able to transform "prose [that] plods from one drab word to the next, all of them pedestrians"[4] into prose that strides with energy and purpose. They can spot the holes, the non sequiturs, the flabby phrases, the disparities and unclarities that even the best writer sometimes cannot see when the story in question is his or her own.

5. Don't take it personally.

Above all, try to remove your ego from your story during the editing process. All writers, even the most experienced, tend to view their stories as little pieces of their own psyches, put out there on display for the world to appreciate.

148

Remember that *you* are not your story. That when an editor is critiquing and criticizing your story, he or she is not attacking *you*. That when the editor says "this is confusing," or "that just doesn't work," he or she is not evaluating your IQ, your personality, even your talent; undoubtedly, he or she is not even *thinking* about your personality, your IQ, or your talent. An editor at work on a story has very narrow tunnel vision: the main concern is how to get the story in shape, how to make it work, how to adapt it to fit the publication. In short, the story is what is on the editor's mind, not you.

Editors are surprised when, in the middle of their attempts to articulate a problem in a story, the beginning writer suddenly bursts into tears (writers of both sexes have been known to do this); or when they happen to glance up and see that the writer's face has turned ghostly pale, or burning red.

One editor, busily explaining the technical problems in a medical story to a writer, failed to notice the young man's increasing silence. Engrossed in the editing, the editor was amazed when the writer suddenly stood up, walked to the side of the editor's desk, and threw up in the wastebasket.

To an editor, a story is an object to be weighed and evaluated against other objects. To a writer, a story on which he or she has labored for days, weeks, or months is no longer an object, but is assimilated and absorbed until it is a subjective part of his or her being.

Burn it into your brain: *Never take editing personally.* This takes a lot of practice, but after years of writing you may, in fact, achieve it.

6. Believe in yourself.

Many stories need to be taken apart, reorganized, and rewritten. Some need to be rewritten more than once. This holds true for famous and experienced writers as well as novices. Don't be impatient or overly critical of yourself.

Don't be impatient or overly critical of yourself—
believe in yourself.

As every successful writer knows:

Revision is democracy's literary method, the tool that allows
an ordinary person to aspire to extraordinary achievement.[5]

EXERCISES

Information is easily available at the click of a mouse, but
how do you filter it to find the solid facts and background you
are looking for? In your research, how do you distinguish
between an accurate source and an unreliable one, between
verifiable fact and speculation?

The exercises below include strategies and sources used by
professional reporters, writers, and researchers—the "secret
weapons" that save time and give extra credibility to your
story. They are a mix of free Web resources and both online
and offline databases that many libraries subscribe to—either
through remote access or at their location.

1. The Web

   When you need to rely on free and easily available
   information sources, you can improve the reliability of
   your Web search through the simple search technique in
   this exercise.

   To begin, assume you are doing a feature on how to eat
   healthier. Do the following searches looking for useful
   background information on nutrition.

   In a search engine type in: nutrition

   a. Assess the top ten hits.

   b. How many do you judge are providing neutral, reli-
      able information that will be useful to your story?
      How many are selling an idea, service, or product?

   Now do a second search.

   Type in: nutrition site:.gov (*exactly* as you see it here).

150

a. Assess the top ten hits.

b. What differences do you see between your first and second searches?

c. If you would like, repeat the same exercises using the suffixes .edu and .org (e.g., nutrition site:.edu, and then nutrition site:.org). Each one will generate a different set of options.

d. Repeat this exercise using a one-word term that applies to research for a story you are writing or would like to write.

   Which search method provides the most useful hits for your research, and why?

2. Web-Based Learning
   The Web offers good tools for teaching how to develop these research skills. One free example is the "mini course" called F.I.R.S.T.: Finding It! offered by the University of North Carolina, Greensboro (http://library.uncg.edu/depts/ref/tutorial/).

3. Powerful Research Favorites for Writers
   These eight basic sources are among the most reliable and popular research tools used by professional writers.

   • CQ Researcher
   • Roper Center for Public Opinion Archives
   • Info Please
   • Encyclopedia of Associations
   • UN Data
   • FedStats
   • International Who's Who
   • Dictionary of Literary Biography

   Using four of the above sources:

   a. Go online and see what they offer.

   b. Write a 25–50 word description of the type of content in each source. Find out whether it is free or requires a paid subscription.

c. Give an example of one way you could use this source for future stories.

4. Revved Up Search Engines and Databases
These are search mega-tools, purchased by libraries and by the pros. Using them will help your writing be more credible, polished, and competitive. The best-known include:

- LexisNexis

- Proquest

- Newsbank

- Readers Guide to Periodical Literature

Do a search in each of these. To gain access, go to your school or public library. If one or more is not available, talk with a librarian, who will help pick an alternate database.

a. Describe in 25–50 words the scope of each and how they differ from Web search tools.

b. Write down and review the search terms you use. Which are most effective and why?

c. Write down the citation (author, publication, date, pages) for one relevant article. This is the kind of information an editor or fact-checker may request.

NOTES

[1] Anna Quindlen, "Times Talk" (in-house publication of *The New York Times*), February 1983.

[2] *Writers at Work:* The Paris Review *Interviews*, George Plimpton, Ed. (New York: Viking Press). Norman Mailer is in the Third Series (1967). Ernest Hemingway is in the Second Series (1963). *The Paris Review,* founded in Paris in 1953, continues to give us "invaluable conversations with the greatest writers of our age."

[3] David Huddle, *The New York Times Book Review,* January 31, 1988.

[4] John Leonard, *The New York Times*, September 2, 1977.

[5] David Huddle, Op. cit.

Freelancing

Every successful writer has learned the ropes of how to get published, get paid, and even earn a good (occasionally great) living based on words. Freelance writing is a good way to get started down this path. You may not get paid for your first published articles, but you will get valuable clips to build your portfolio. (The term "clips" originates in predigital days, when writers saved their stories by clipping them from hard copy publications.)

The range of freelance outlets is vast, both in print and online.

On Spec vs. On Assignment

Where to start? Freelance writers take varied approaches to marketing their work. Most start with smaller digital or printed publications and then target ones with bigger audiences as they get published; some start by pitching to their dream publication even knowing that rejection is probable. Deciding which strategy to use depends on your story idea and its potential audience.

There are two traditional ways to market a story: you can write it either on speculation ("on spec"), or on assignment.

To write *on spec* means you have an idea, you query an editor, and she or he likes the idea and promises to consider your finished manuscript for publication. The editor has no *obligation* to publish it. The writer takes all the chances. You are more likely to be asked to write on spec when starting out. While not all publications offer this option, many do. It is a painless way for publications to give you a chance to prove yourself.

To write *on assignment* means you have an idea, you query an editor about it—either in an informal conversation, or in a formal written proposal—and the editor agrees to publish the story. This means that, barring unforeseen hitches, the editor has a commitment—perhaps legal, at least ethical—to publish. The writer's risk is reduced. You are more likely to be given assignments—backed up with a written confirmation of the terms— once you are a published writer with a proven track record.

Even for those who want to be writers for major publications, starting with smaller digital or print publications is often a good way to begin to get clips, which will help you get assignments later. Editors at community newspapers and smaller Web sites are often hungry for fresh ideas and good writers. As a result, these editors are more likely to give you a chance. Be forewarned, however, that small newspapers/magazines and Web sites may pay you nothing, or barely enough to buy pizza for friends. But most writers start out small (both in terms of audience and income for their stories) and work their way up. The important thing in the beginning is to accumulate clips and a track record of productive working relationships with professional editors.

If you cannot draw the interest of an established editor-monitored publication, you can publish in your school newspaper or magazine, or on a plethora of smaller Web sites and blogs that welcome unsolicited content if it fits their market (see chapter 10).

You can also publish your own blog—which can be a useful prelude to publishing in established media. If the writing and reporting on your blog are strong enough, it can become your "calling card," a place to direct editors even if you have no other published clips. A quality blog can show your skills, style, and potential (see chapter 10). For most writers, how-ever, the ultimate goal is to appear in established forums that pay, which is the focus of this chapter.

Finding the Right Market: Three Steps to Success

Once you have an idea for a story, it is crucial to *tailor the story* for a specific publication.

First, study the publications for which you want to write, and read them on a regular basis. Be familiar with their con-tent. Nothing will kill your publication chances faster than to propose an idea and be told by the editor: if you read us, you would know we (a) did that story six months ago or (b) never do that kind of story. In many ways this is easier to do than ever before, as most publications have Web sites with archived material. Use the search box on the site to see if they have cov-ered your topic before.

Second, look closely at how content is organized in the publication. Longer feature stories appear in the main edito-rial "well" of print magazines, and are headlined on the home pages of digital media. These are generally written by estab-lished writers. The best approach for new writers is to propose briefer articles such as those found in the "front-of-book" sec-tions of magazines and the special sections of Web sites.

Magazines that publish personal essays also offer publica-tion opportunities for writers who are less established. If you are a first-time writer you will probably need to write the per-sonal essay in full before submitting it, but if your subject and tone feel right to the editor you might just hit a home run.

Another approach is to think about the people to whom you have access. Is there anyone in your personal or profes-sional life who is well-known or well-placed in their field who might make an interesting subject for an article? Just the fact

155

that you know this person and can arrange an interview with them may be enough to be considered for assignment.

Third, be efficient (and make your life easier) by going to sources that will help you match your story ideas with the best market. Go online or take advantage of your local library, where research professionals can direct you to the more expensive (and comprehensive) online and hard copy sources the library subscribes to so you don't have to pay for access. The tried-and-true, and still most popular, sources include:

- *Writer's Market: Where & How To Sell What You Write.* This classic online and printed guide has more than 3,500 listings of magazines (with a freelance rate chart), book publishers, and even literary agents. It includes information on how to write query letters, read contracts, promote yourself, and launch your own freelance business.

- *Gale Directory of Publications and Broadcast Media.* This useful online and printed reference contains thousands of contact names of editors and producers in print media, radio, TV, and cable stations. It includes e-mail and physical addresses, phone and fax numbers, key personnel, and owner names.

You can, of course, go straight to the Web and get access to a free treasure trove of useful information. It is with some trepidation that specific Web sites are recommended, because of the pace at which sites come and go, or morph their content in order to attract more advertisers and readers. With that proviso, here are two worth checking out:

- **Mediabistro.com** is loaded with advice from editors about how to pitch them for work (sample: target a specific section of the magazine or Web site; send a quick query by e-mail), and from freelancers about their experiences with specific print and digital publications. Some media also use the site to find available freelancers, and for a fee you can post your writing credentials.

- **Mastheads.org** is a collaborative, community-based directory of 750+ magazine staff mastheads, updated regularly.

Once you have taken the first steps, contact the publication you have in mind and verify with an assistant the name, spelling, and title of the editor who is in charge of the section you want to query. Editors tend to change jobs frequently, and the information you have may be outdated. Be sure to get off to a good start by making your pitch to the right person.

Querying the Editor

A query is a brief written proposal that captures the essence of your story, your approach, and your writing style. Check the publication's Web site, or sites for freelancers like those above, for instructions on how it prefers to receive freelance queries.

The Phone Call

Editors generally do not like phone calls from writers wanting to pitch a story. As one editor (who has also been a freelance writer) explains: "Editors are so, so busy that it would feel too nervy if an unknown writer called me and wanted to take my time. First, how can I know if that person can write?"

Established writers have more leeway. Once you have developed a track record of quality published writing, it is sometimes fine to call an editor who knows your published work—or, better yet, has published you before—to touch base and ask if they would be interested in receiving a query from you on a given topic.

E-mail

Most editors prefer an e-mail query. For the editor, the e-mail advantage is convenience. He or she can then consider your written proposal as soon as they have time, see how succinctly you can write, and share your e-mail with other editors who will be involved in the decision-making.

For you, the e-mail advantage is that it forces you to develop a brief and snappy summary of your story. It also gives you a written record of the date and content of the query. Keep it brief, and include it in the body of the e-mail. If you need to put your query in an attachment because of its length, it is too long. If you want to put it in an attachment anyway, then give the nugget of it in the e-mail, so the editor is intrigued enough to take that extra step to open it.

Writing the Query

The writing of a query is an art in itself. The query is, basically, a press release for your story: it has to *sell* the story to your editor. Your own query should do the following:

Be Brief

As an editor of *The New York Times Magazine* once explained, "Great minds have short attention spans." Most editors want you to demonstrate in your query the ability to concisely state your idea. If your story can't be summarized in three or four sentences, the thinking goes, it probably has not been fully thought through.

Be Polished

The query must be addressed to the right person, with the correct title and name *spelled correctly without any variations whatsoever.* Don't assume Ann Marie is spelled Anne-Marie.

In the subject line, type "query on" followed by a three- or four-word description of your pitch. Because this is your first chance to grab the editor's attention, make sure the subject line is simple and direct. The query must contain no typos or grammatical errors. Otherwise, chances are great your e-mail will be sent to the trash.

Be Snappy

Once an editor opens your e-mail, you have at most ten seconds to grab her or his attention, so carefully craft the first sentence of your query. Be clear about the subject matter, but be creative. An intriguing question, an interesting fact, a quote from someone you interviewed, an anecdote, or a gripping statistic can be useful because it shows your writing style. Sometimes the compelling lead of your feature will also work as the first sentence or paragraph of the query.

Outline Your Approach

Tell the editor in the query *exactly* what you plan to cover in the story, and how you plan to do it. Be clear about your focus in order to minimize future misunderstandings about the scope or tone of the story. Be as specific as possible to show that you have done your homework and are not just floating a random idea. Briefly mention the names or types of people you plan to interview and summarize the research you have done and plan to do.

*Once an editor opens your e-mail,
you have at most ten seconds to grab her or his attention.*

Be Appropriate

Write the query in the style of the publication to which you are submitting it: this shows that you know not only the content but also the tone of the publication. Make it clear that you know the target audience. Before you send the query, read back issues to be sure that the publication has not recently covered the same topic.

Be Self-Confident

Avoid query letters that begin: "I don't know if you'll be interested in this, but . . ." or "I've never published before, but. . . ." Sell your competence in your query.

Give Your Credentials

At the *end,* explain briefly why you have special knowledge, access, insight, or background in this story. If you spent your vacation mountain biking in the Rockies and your story idea is about mountain biking, be sure to mention your experience since it gives authority to your pitch. If you have clips, provide them. If you have a good blog, give the link. If you have not published, give whatever credentials you have that are relevant.

Omit Business Details

Do not bring up issues of payment, copyright, expenses, deadline, or any of the other nitty-gritty details. They will come up later if the editor is interested.

End Gracefully

Tell the editor that you look forward to speaking with her or him about the story. Include your name, e-mail and physical addresses, and phone numbers at the end of the query.

The Follow-Up

Some writers note at the end of the query that they will follow up with the editor in, say, two weeks. If you include such a statement, then follow up as promised. A brief, polite e-mail may be enough to jog an answer and can alleviate a lot of second guessing. The longer the publication takes to respond, the less likely it is that the editor is enthusiastic about the idea. However, be patient. Responses also get delayed by e-mails lost in cyberspace, the need for multiple editors to review and approve your piece, vacations, illness, or even a change of staff or owners.

Know When To Move On

If one or two follow-ups bring no positive response, then just quietly give up. Repeated follow-ups will become annoying. If a new writer gets known for being a pest, it can be the "kiss of death" for her or his future with the publication. Go ahead and send the query to the next publication. The worst that can happen is that two publications will want to buy your story. The odds are greatly against this, however. It almost never happens. The fact is that most story ideas *are* rejected, which is why some people who are trying to make a living by freelance writing develop several different story ideas so they can send out multiple queries on different topics to different publications at one time.

Sometimes a writer trying to break into the freelance market will send out the same query on the same idea to multiple publications at one time. This is obviously to the writer's advantage, since it saves a lot of time waiting for a linear series of rejections. Most editors, however, feel this is an unfair practice and a sign of an amateur writer who is unfamiliar with the protocols of publishing. Each editor likes to retain the unique right to review your query, and reject or accept your idea.

If you want to send out simultaneous queries on the same topic, you should as a professional courtesy let each editor know.

Editors, of course, do not face similar constraints. They have the right to consider several queries on similar or related topics, choose one writer to handle the story, and then give that writer "advice" for the approach based in part on the other queries that were rejected. This is one of the inequities faced by freelance feature writers. You have to decide for yourself which routes you want to take, but always keep in mind your long-term reputation for professionalism.

Trust Editors

Beginning writers sometimes worry that if they send in a query their idea will be stolen outright and given to another writer. While an editor may "spin off" a query, and consciously or subconsciously pass information along to another writer who may be working on the same topic, it is rare—surprisingly rare, in fact—for publications to outright steal ideas. When it does happen, it may result in a lawsuit, with the publication paying damages to a writer who can prove the idea was stolen. The problem is that so few ideas are unique: chances are your wonderful idea is someone else's wonderful idea as well. When topics become "hot," editors are not only flooded with queries related to them, but are also making their own assignments on these topics to writers whose work they know.

Your challenge—as new writer on the block—is to craft such a compelling query that it outshines the others. If an editor is impressed with the writing in your query but not with the partic-

Few ideas are unique. Chances are your wonderful idea is someone else's wonderful idea as well.

ular idea, the editor will usually encourage you to submit other ideas. You should do so, until you finally get an assignment.

Your Rights and Responsibilities

Every time you sell an article as a freelancer, you have entered into a unique business agreement. It may be in the form of a legal contract, or a letter from the editor to you or from you to the editor (called a "letter of agreement"). In some cases—with smaller newspapers and magazines or Web sites—the agreement may be verbal. It is a good idea, however, to take notes during the conversation and send the editor an e-mail confirming the details, in case of future misunderstandings about the terms of the assignment.

Contracts

Contracts are often filled with a dizzying array of legalese and strange terms: First North American Serial rights, First Print Rights, First Electronic Rights, Work for Hire.[1] Do you sign the contract (and possibly give up all your rights of ownership) or do you start crossing out stipulations with the hopes of keeping some ownership of the piece?

The reality is that new, unknown writers have little to no leverage to modify a publication's standard contract. It usually will not hurt to ask, but be prepared to give in graciously for the sake of building the relationship. With more credentials, contract issues can sometimes, but not always, become more negotiable.

There is no one-size-fits-all answer for what to keep and what to cross out in a contract or letter of agreement. This has always been true, and is more so even now as writers' rights are in a state of flux with the rise of digital media and the volatility and vulnerability of the media industry. Find a mentor in the form of an experienced writer or editor (teachers and professors of writing often have these credentials) and seek advice based on your particular circumstance. Also go to the Web sites of professional writers' groups who follow contract issues, such as the American Society of Journalists and Authors (ASJA) and The National Writer's Union.

Your Ethical Responsibilities

One aspect of freelancing that is not in flux is your responsibility as a writer to act with integrity. Never plagiarize. Never fabricate. New writers can be a bit hazy about the parameters of these responsibilities. Know them well, for if violated they are career-enders.

Plagiarism

A good definition of plagiarism (a euphemism for stealing) is:

> Attempting to pass off someone else's words or ideas as your own without proper attribution or acknowledgment. In both journalism and academia, this is akin to theft. Examples: Copying in whole or in part a published article or another student's paper, borrowing language or concepts, lifting quotes or failing to use quotation marks where appropriate.[2]

Fabrication

A useful definition of fabrication (a euphemism for lying) is: "Making up information, faking anecdotes or sources, falsifying quotes, creating fictitious sources, citing non-existent articles, or fudging data."[3]

You must be able to verify that all the information you present in your articles is factual and correct, that it is from

164

your own reporting, and that you have documentation. Some publications employ fact checkers to verify the original source of every fact in an article, including checking quotes with sources. You should maintain that standard yourself whether or not there is a fact checker. Anything in quote marks is expected to be what the sources said, and not edited in any way that could change their meaning. If you use previously published quotes (which you should lean on as little as possible—do your own reporting) you must attribute them to the original source.

If you cannot distinguish in your notes which information you gathered first hand and which you gathered from an online site, then do not use it. Many reporters have lost their jobs—and their future as writers—because they carelessly or intentionally used other people's work and presented it as their own. Your byline carries with it your reputation for integrity.

EXERCISES

1. Identify three publications that have both digital and print versions. Compare them.

   a. How is their content the same and how does it differ?

   b. What is the difference in format?

   c. What is the difference in word count?

   d. What information is provided for contacting an editor and submitting a query?

   e. Which publication would you prefer to query? Why?

2. Develop for two publications two different queries that have a cultural, social, or political "angle" that would interest their editors. Over the course of the next few classes:

   a. Describe and refine your idea in class.

   b. Research the idea so you have context and data (statistics, prevalence of trend or issue, etc.).

c. Write a 50–100 word query targeted to each publication's style and audience.

3. Now comes the reality check.

a. Pair off in class and exchange one of your queries.

b. Role play, with one student taking the part of the writer, and one the editor. In 60 seconds, the writer makes the pitch, and the editor (kindly but succinctly) asks questions and decides whether the query is suitable for his or her publication.

c. Now switch roles, using the other student's query for the pitch.

d. Under the direction of the instructor, share in class what you learned from this exercise about query writing and about the role of the editor.

4. Submit your query to the publication and share what you learned—and the outcome—with the class.

NOTES

[1] See Allena Tapia, Know Your Publication Rights: What Exactly Are You Selling, http://freelancewrite.about.com/od/legalissues/a/rights.htm

[2] Ethics Pledge, New York University, Arthur L. Carter Journalism Institute, 2008, http://journalism.nyu.edu/ethics/

[3] Ibid.

Writing for the Web: Six Tools for Success

Writing for the Web requires the same knowledge of and sensitivity to the power of words as described in prior chapters.

However, the way you grab readers and keep their attention is different. It is important that you understand these differences, and how to use them to help showcase your own feature writing.

Here are six tools to help guide you to success.

1. Know What Web Readers Want

The person who willingly spends ten minutes reading your well-crafted and compelling story in a printed publication does not have the same level of patience on the Web.

This is because the intent and attention span of Web readers—whether they are visiting an established online publication or a newcomer blog—are different.

- **Intent.** Most Web readers are goal-driven. They do not like to linger. They go to the Web looking for specific information that is personally useful or important. This affects their reading behavior.

- **Attention span.** Studies by Web usability expert Jakob Nielsen and others show that Web readers scan text—skimming it rather than reading word for word as they do in a newspaper, magazine, or book that is printed or downloaded to a digital reader for perusing at their leisure.

On the Web, readers may give your story five seconds of their time—if you are lucky. Time-pressed, or unimpressed by what you are offering, they are going to click, click, click off pages that don't highlight the information they are seeking.

This difference in intent and attention span has a lot to do with the medium of the Web itself. In traditional media formats—print, TV, radio, and movies—people are willing to let the "creator"—the writer or director—take the lead, while they come along for the ride. They are comfortable as spectators to someone else's creation.

But the Web is different. It is interactive, not passive. It is multitask-friendly. It invites users to engage and share, to make active choices, to scroll, navigate, link, copy, paste, print, post, and send to friends.

Your challenge as a writer is to give your audience "content"—i.e., your story—that is succinct, specific, and useful. Content that will catch and hold their attention.

2. Know What Web Editors Want

Readers can scan, click, and leave; but if you are to succeed as a writer, you must do your research the old-fashioned way—by spending time digging around.

It is important for you as a writer to get to know the sites you plan to approach with a story idea. Scrutinize, analyze, learn by example. Become familiar with the content, tone, style, length, and format of their material (see chapter 9).

Publishers can track their readers' interests far more specifically on their Web sites than they can for their printed publications. Using advanced analytics tools, professional Web sites continually track their readers' habits—who is on the site, how long they stay on an article, where they go next.

Editors expect you, their writer, to be aware of this and emulate their style and format. The same holds true whether it is a continually updated news site, an online monthly magazine, or a blog. (For how to create your own blog, see pages 173–176.)

168

3. Modify How You Present Your Story

Keeping your Web readers in mind, follow these guidelines when crafting your story.

- **Use a summation lead.** This traditional news-style lead gives readers the key facts and context at the top, which is important on the Web (see chapter 1). If you want to use an irresistible feature lead, then be sure your headline says exactly what the story is about.

- **Keep paragraphs short.** Web readers click away from large blocks of text. It is better if you break your paragraphs into two to three sentences each. This may involve adding a transition word or phrase to lead off the next paragraph. If possible, present one idea/concept per paragraph.

- **Maintain crisp, clear language.** Be vivid and concise. Make your sentences short.

- **Write your own headings.** Headings and subheadings are guideposts-at-a-glance to your story. They also help break up blocks of text.

  Apply a bold font that is one to two points larger than the main text. Keep headings and subheadings brief—optimal length is one to three words. Make them simple and direct. Do not be cutesy or metaphorical, or you will lose your reader.

  Do not rely on your Web editor (if there is one) to do this for you. You know your story best. If you have an editor, she or he will appreciate your effort, and may have better suggestions.

- **Highlight "key words" for search engine optimization.** Readers looking for the topic you are writing about put "key words" into a search engine. When the results

169

direct them to the page with your story, they will scan the page looking for those same words.

If your topic is the 2010 BP oil spill in the Gulf of Mexico, highlight "**oil spill**" and **"Gulf Coast"** high up in your story. Make them pop off the page to draw the reader's eye.

Highlighted words also help break up large blocks of text. Be careful to not highlight too much—a few words every three to four paragraphs is usually enough to be enticing without being intrusive.

- **Keep your story under 600 words.** Studies show that Web readers do not stick around for pages that scroll on and on. For the luxury of longer stories, there are appealing alternate ways to layer your text. Follow the arrow.

4. Think Visually

There are many ways to keep a reader's interest by combining text and visuals. On a professionally maintained site, editors will make these decisions for you. On your own Web site, it is up to you. You can try the following.[1]

- **Create listicles.** Listicles (the word is a combination of "lists" and "article") are excerpts from your piece that lend themselves to being broken out in list form. The listicle can highlight data, quotes, or other information. If the story is long and jumps to another page, a listicle can be used as a table of contents for the entire story. Use

Listicles are excerpts that lend themselves to being broken out in list form.

bullet points or other graphic elements (a lightly shaded box under a listicle can be good as long as it is not too dark) to draw the reader's eye and help differentiate it from the main text.

- **Pull out quotes.** Extract the best quotes that are buried inside your story, and feature them as a separate graphic element on the page. You can increase the font size, change the color, surround them with white space and—voila! You have a useful design element.

- **Create sidebars.** You may be able to shape a description or anecdote you have woven into your story into its own enticing mini-story for your readers. Be sure to give the sidebar its own header.

- **Use photos or charts with captions.** Graphics help tell your story in another way. They also give you another opportunity to transfer some of the text out of your story (i.e., reduce its length) and put it instead in an explanatory caption under the graphic, where it is more likely to be read.

- **Use second-level navigation.** On professional Web sites, you will notice that longer and more prominent stories usually jump from its home page to a second-level "destination" page. This allows the writer to continue the story on a new screen—which is preferable to the endless scroll down a single page. If the reader is "hooked" so far, they will happily click through.

  Once readers go to that page, don't let them down. Use the same appealing graphic elements and design as you did on the home page.

- **Be interactive.** Link to audio, video, photos, or other graphics that are elsewhere on the site, or are on other Web sites. They should amplify and expand your story; do not rely on them to provide core information that should be in the body of your text.

Always make it clear where the link is leading. For example, "A Census Bureau report on teen pregnancy . . ." link is better than one that says "A recent study found. . . ." Don't link whole sentences—only the key words.

Don't be afraid to link to other sites, thinking that your reader will leave and never return. Web readers expect links, and if they find yours useful, they will click back to you for more.

5. Deliver Quality

Tight transitions, strong verbs, a compelling quote, and the apt description (as described in prior chapters) are even more important in the fast-moving, expansive, fragmented Web environment.

This ability to create and control your "voice" (see chapter 6) is critical for the Web.

You have an edge over most Web writers if you understand and deploy your arsenal of best writing techniques. They generate the energy that drives the power of your words and makes people want to read you.

6. Focus on Your Fundamentals

Because there are fewer "gatekeepers" and editors on the Web to help catch embarrassing errors, be sure to check for them yourself. Especially:

- **Spelling and typos.** Use spell checker and online dictionaries (is it "opthamology or ophthalmology"? "Colombia" or "Columbia"?). Always double-check—especially if you are sure that you are right.

- **Grammar.** Watch your grammar (is it "affect" or "effect"? "compose" or "comprise"?). Unintentional misuse of grammar undermines your message and drives readers away.

172

- **Punctuation.** Even the best-known, most-famous writers can miss a period at the end of a sentence, or forget to put a "closing quote mark at the end of the quote. (Guilty here, as charged.) If your mistake causes confusion, Web readers will look for a story that is easier to follow.

- **Accuracy.** Fact-checking tends to be less rigorous on the Web than in print. Even large publishing companies that do fact-check their online publications may use standards that are different for the Web. This makes you more vulnerable to publishing wrong information, which, in the Web environment, is more likely to go viral and cause you grief.

  Writers are liable for their own factual errors—whether online or offline. But in traditional media, there are often more layers of editors who, in the slower production process, have time to check and catch mistakes.

  Cover your butt. Be sure you can attribute your facts to valid original sources.

- **Proofing.** Before posting or submitting your story for review, proofread your work with a fresh eye. It is recommended that you print your story and proof from the hard copy. Mistakes are often easier to miss on screen than when you see them on the printed page.

Creating Your Own Blog

The blog—the name is a blend of "web" and "log"—is a type of Web site usually created as a forum for opinions, facts, and/or a presentation of specific materials. Blogging has become a favored method of self-publishing, and can provide an aspiring feature writer with a useful stage on which to showcase their materials. A well-written blog can become your "calling card," a place to direct readers and potential editors.

While social networking sites may serve well enough for posting your stories for friends, a stand-alone blog gives you a more professional image.

How To Get Started

A blog is relatively easy to set up. Nearly 60 percent of bloggers create their own blog by using a free third-party hosting service.[2] Search for "how to create your own blog" to find Web sites that will get you started. For your writing career, be sure to set up a professional blog, not one that functions as an online diary.

Decide on Your Focus—Wide or Narrow

A *wide-ranging* blog works well when you are a new writer, or a student in a writing class, and you plan to showcase your talents across different topics.

You can post a variety of stories to show your range of style, such as longer features, brief interviews, or comments with links to related sources.

If you are taking writing classes—whether feature writing, journalism, magazine, English, or any other writing genre—a blog is a good way to "repurpose" your class assignments rather than leave them, neglected and unread, on your computer. By the end of the semester, you will have a range of posts and completed articles.

Once you get started, the very process of blogging also helps you hone your research and reporting skills. Once you post your article, you will often see new ways in which you can add depth and perspective.

A *narrow blog* focuses on one topic. If you choose a narrow focus, it is important to keep on top of what else is being published. To do this, set up your own "beat" (a publishing term for writers assigned to cover one specific topic). Search engines such as Google and Bing offer free "alerts," or links, to all relevant stories, delivered daily to your e-mail. You can browse through them, post a brief comment, and link to the article.

Name Your Blog

The name you choose should be specific rather than generic, brief, easy to remember, and reflect the content. Some people include their own name as part of the blog name. It is a good idea to also include a key word that search engines are likely to pick up.

Make It Look Good

Just as with any Web site, your blog needs not only good writing but also good graphics. Take a camera with you on assignments and shoot photos, audio, and/or video depending on the requirements of the story. Cell phone technology for photos and video is improving and it can be an alternative to carrying a separate camera. If you shoot enough visuals, there are likely to be a few that are suitable for your blog. You can also download and post photos and graphics from sites that offer royalty free, noncopyrighted, professional photographs.

Go Viral

If you want your blog to serve as your calling card and entrée into paid assignments, then it is important to show editors that your work can draw readers.

You can promote your blog by linking and commenting at related sites and sites that show up on your daily alerts. The goal is get your blog cruising down a two-way street with you linking and commenting at other sites and vice versa.

Promote your blog on social networking media (Twitter and Facebook currently dominate the market). On Twitter, the tweets you send are only available to those who follow you, but you can share your blog's url (which stands for uniform resource locator) with everyone, and generate your own built-in audience. It is also a fast way to feel the pulse of breaking news, find additional sources, keep track of your beat, and get ideas and feedback.

Your well-done blog should be linked at the end of an e-mail query to an editor (see chapter 9). The editor will see that you have a demonstrated interest in and knowledge of the topic.

Digital Media: The Beginning of the Future

As a writer, it is good to keep in mind that the Web and other digital media have altered but not replaced prior channels of communication. Newspapers, magazines, and books are still prevalent, however, the medium they appear in is shape shifting, making an unobstructed view of their future difficult at best.

Just as TV did not replace radio, and radio did not replace print, so too the Web site structure itself, along with its current offspring (such as social networking media), are just our most recent, most powerful, and newest tools for telling our stories.[3]

Enjoy. Adapt. Write well and prosper.

EXERCISES

1. Describe the specific ways in which the writing and presentation in this chapter differs from earlier chapters. Assess what the reader gains and loses by this difference.

2. Take the most recent story you have written for class or a printed publication. Adapt it for the Web. Post it on your school's Web site, a blog, or a social networking site.

   a. What elements were you able to use?

   b. What elements did you discard, and why?

   c. What do you like and want to improve about the end result?

   d. What are the advantages and disadvantages of the way you presented the story in each medium?

3. Find a 1,000–1,500 word feature story published by another writer in a newspaper or magazine that has *also* been published on the Web.

   a. What are the differences and similarities in style and presentation?

   b. Which do you think is more effective, and why?

   c. Assess what the reader gains and loses in terms of content and context on each medium.

4. Start your own blog.

   a. Go to Technorati.com, Bloggerschoiceawards.com, PCmagazine.com, or Time.com/best25blogs and look at their list of top blogs.

   b. Choose four blogs that appeal to you.

      • Analyze each for focus, content, writing style, format, and user-friendliness.

      • Identify the *common factors* that qualify them as "top" level blogs.

      • Discuss which blog most appeals to you, and why.

   c. Use what you have learned from this chapter and your own analysis to help formulate your focus for your own blog.

NOTES

[1] For more on how to attract and keep readers' attention, go to Web usability expert Jakob Nielsen's site at www.useit.com. Also search for "best writing for the Web."

[2] Matt Sussman, The How of Blogging, June 4, 2010, in State of the Blogosphere 2009, Technorati.com. Among other services, Technorati is an aggregator of information on blogging and other social networking.

[3] As intelligent computing gains more traction in the Web world, the notion of clicking on individual Web addresses to reach information—and even the concept of using a specific "browser" as the engine to get there—will be transformed. If you are interested in knowing more about what lies ahead for the Web, and how it might impact your role as a writer, search for "future Web trends."

The APME Association's
"50 Common Errors in Newspaper Writing"

In 1974 the Writing and Editing Committee of the Associated Press Managing Editors Association published "50 Common Errors in Newspaper Writing." It is still a classic, providing basic rules of grammar that are often neglected or overlooked. A complete list first appeared in *Editor & Publisher.* Here is a sample:

Affect, effect. Generally, *affect* is the verb; *effect* is the noun. "The letter did not *affect* the outcome." "The letter had a significant *effect.*" BUT *effect* is also a verb meaning *to bring about.* Thus: "It is almost impossible to *effect* change."

Allude, elude. You *allude* to (or mention) a book. You *elude* (or escape) a pursuer.

Annual. Don't use *first* with it. If it's the first time, it can't be annual.

Averse, adverse. If you don't like something, you are *averse* (or opposed) to it. *Adverse* is an adjective: *adverse* (bad) weather, *adverse* conditions.

Compose, comprise. Remember that the parts *compose* the whole and the whole is *comprised* of the parts. You *compose* things by putting them together. Once the parts are put together, the object comprises or is *comprised* of the parts.

Demolish, destroy. They mean to do away with *completely.* You can't partially demolish or destroy something, nor is there any need to say *totally* destroyed.

Different from. Things and people are different *from* each other. Don't write that they are different *than* each other.

Drown. Don't say someone was *drowned* unless an assailant held the victim's head under water. Just say the victim *drowned.*

Ecology, environment. They are not synonymous. *Ecology* is the study of the relationship between organisms and their *environment.*

    Right: The laboratory is studying the *ecology* of man and the desert.

    Right: There is much interest in animal *ecology* these days.

    Wrong: Even so simple an undertaking as maintaining a lawn affects *ecology.*

    Right: Even so simple an undertaking as maintaining a lawn affects our *environment.*

Either. It means one or the other, not both.

    Wrong: There were lions on *either* side of the door.

    Right: There were lions on *each* side of the door.

Flout, flaunt. They aren't the same words; they mean completely different things and they're very commonly confused. *Flout* means to mock, to scoff, or to show disdain for. *Flaunt* means to display ostentatiously.

Funeral service. A redundant expression. A funeral *is* a service.

Head up. People don't *head up* committees. They *head* them.

Hopefully. One of the most commonly misused words, in spite of what the dictionary may say. *Hopefully* should describe the way the subject *feels.* For instance: Hopefully, I shall present the plan to the president. (This means I will be hopeful when I do it.) But it is something else again when you attribute hope to a non-person. You might write: Hopefully, the war will end soon. This means you hope the war will end soon, but it is not what you are writing. What you mean is: I hope the war will end soon.

Imply, infer. The speaker implies. The hearer infers.

Lay, lie. *Lay* is the action word; *lie* is the state of being.

    Wrong: The body will *lay* in state until Wednesday.

    Right: The body will *lie* in state until Wednesday.

    Right: The prosecutor tried to *lay* the blame on him.

    However, the past tense of *lie* is *lay.*

    Right: The body *lay* in state from Tuesday until Wednesday.

    Wrong: The body *laid* in state from Tuesday until Wednesday.

The past participle and the plain past tense of *lay* is *laid*.

Right: He *laid* the pencil on the pad.

Right: He *had laid* the pencil on the pad.

Right: The hen *laid* an egg.

Leave, let: *Leave alone* means to depart from or cause to be in solitude. *Let alone* means to be undisturbed.

Wrong: The man had pulled a gun on her but Mr. Jones intervened and talked him into *leaving her alone*.

Right: The man had pulled a gun on her but Mr. Jones intervened and talked him into *letting her alone*.

Right: When I entered the room I saw that Jim and Mary were sleeping so I decided to *leave them alone*.

Less, fewer. If you can separate items in the quantities being compared, use *fewer*. If not, use *less*.

Wrong: The Rams are inferior to the Vikings because they have *less* good linemen.

Right: The Rams are inferior to the Vikings because they have *fewer* good linemen.

Right: The Rams are inferior to the Vikings because they have *less* experience.

Like, as. Don't use *like* for *as* or *as if*. In general, use *like* to compare with nouns and pronouns; use *as* when comparing with phrases and clauses that contain a verb.

Wrong: Jim blocks the linebacker *like* he should.

Right: Jim blocks the linebacker *as* he should.

Right: Jim blocks *like* a pro.

Oral, verbal. Use *oral* when use of the mouth is central to the thought; the word emphasizes the idea of human utterance. *Verbal* may apply to spoken or written words; it connotes the process of reducing ideas to writing. Usually, it's a *verbal* contract, not an *oral* one, if it's in writing.

Over, more than. They aren't interchangeable. *Over* refers to spatial relationships: The plane flew over the city. *More than* is used with figures: In the crowd were more than 1,000 fans.

Principle, principal. A guiding rule or basic truth is a principle. The first, dominant, or leading thing is *principal*. *Principle* is a noun; principal may be a noun or an adjective.

Right: It's the principle of the thing.

Right: Liberty and justice are two *principles* on which our nation is founded.

Right: Hitting and fielding are the *principal* activities in baseball.

Right: Robert Jamieson is the school principal.

Refute. The word connotes success in argument and almost always implies an editorial judgment.

Wrong: Father Bury *refuted* the arguments of the pro-abortion faction.

Right: With the new DNA evidence, the attorney was able to refute her client's guilt.

Reluctant, reticent. If he doesn't want to act, he is *reluctant*. If he doesn't want to speak, he is *reticent*.

That, which. *That* tends to restrict the reader's thought and direct it the way you want it to go; *which* is nonrestrictive, introducing a bit of subsidiary information. For instance:

The lawn mower that is in the garage needs sharpening. (Meaning: We have more than one lawn mower. The one in the garage needs sharpening.)

The lawn mower, which is in the garage, needs sharpening. (Meaning: Our lawn mower needs sharpening. It's in the garage.)

Note that *which* clauses take commas, signaling they are not essential to the meaning of the sentence.

Who, whom. A tough one, but generally you're safe to use *whom* to refer to someone who has been the object of an action. *Who* is the word when the somebody has been the actor:

A 19-year-old woman, to *whom* the room was rented, left the window open.

A 19-year-old woman, *who* rented the room, left the window open.

Who's, whose. Though it incorporates an apostrophe, *who's* is not a possessive. It's a contraction for *who is*. *Whose* is the possessive.

Wrong: I don't know *who's* coat it is.

Right: I don't know *whose* coat it is.

Right: Find out *who's* there.

Index

Accent, foreign, 79–80
Action, 30–31
   compressing, 31–32, 55
   sensitivity to, 6
   verbs conveying, 28–32
Adverbs, 39
American Society of Journalists
   and Authors (ASJA), 164
Anecdotes, 123–125
Antecedents, pronoun agreement
   with, 41–42
Associated Press Managing Edi-
   tors Association (APME), 179
Attribution, 173

Background description, 17, 134
Barzun, Jacques, 41, 114
Blogging, 155, 173–176
Boring but important (BBI) infor-
   mation, 132–134
Brinkley, Christie, 51

Clichés, 104
Closure, 134–136
Colloquialisms, 115
Conjunctions, 19, 22
Contracts, 163–164
Controversy and synopsis, 125–126

Dangling participles, 24
Description, 49–63
   capturing details, 51–54
   of feelings, 58–62

highlighting quotes and tension with, 9
of individuals, 56–57
noticing nuances, 54–55
observation and, 49–51
panoramic, 56
selectivity in, 55–56
showcasing specific persons, 58
and verbs, 28–29
wrapping around strong verbs,
   62–63
Descriptive leads, 5–7
Detail
   attention to, 6
   information gathering and,
   51–55
   See also Description
Didion, Joan, 50, 52, 98, 103

Editing, 146–150
Editors, 157–162
Electric Kool-Aid Acid Test, The
   (Wolfe), 99
Eliot, T. S., 59
Emerson, Ralph Waldo, 59
Emotion, describing, 51. *See also*
   Feelings
Emphatics, 22–23
Ethical responsibilities, 164–165
Exposition, 120

Fabrication, 164–165
Fact-checking, 173

183

184

185